THE DECORATIVE ARTS COLLECTION MUSEUM
PRESENTS

# ORNAMENT
# Extravaganza

A COLLECTION OF PAINTED ORNAMENTS FOR

VALENTINE'S DAY • EASTER • FOURTH OF JULY • HALLOWEEN • CHRISTMAS

Published by:
All American Crafts, Inc.
7 Waterloo Road
Stanhope, NJ 07874
www.allamericancrafts.com

To order the ornament surfaces shown in this book, see Sources on page 125.

Publisher: Jerry Cohen
Chief Executive Officer: Darren Cohen
Product Development Director: Brett Cohen
Art Direction: Andy Jones
Proofreader: Natalie Rhinesmith
Editorial Advisors: Peggy Harris and Linda Heller

# PaintWorks® Quick & Easy Painting

Printed in China
©2010 Decorative Arts Collection Museum, Inc.
ISBN 978-0-9819762-2-8
Library of Congress Control Number 2010922219

# ORNAMENT
## Extravaganza

**T**HANK **YOU** TO THOSE ARTISTS WHO GENEROUSLY DONATED THEIR TIME AND TALENT TO BRING TOGETHER THIS COLLECTION OF ORNAMENTS.

THERE ARE ORNAMENTS AND DECORATIONS TO ENCHANT YOU ALL YEAR LONG — FROM VALENTINE'S DAY ALL THE WAY TO CHRISTMAS. WHETHER DECORATING A TREE, A PACKAGE, OR A SPECIAL NOOK, THEY WILL ADD CHARM TO YOUR DECOR ALL THROUGHOUT THE YEAR!

- LYNNE ANDREWS
- HELAN BARRICK
- TRUDY BEARD
- MARGOT CLARK
- DEBBIE COTTON
- HEIDI ENGLAND
- CYNTHIA EREKSON
- PEGGY HARRIS
- KAREN HUBBARD
- JO SONJA JANSEN
- ANDY JONES
- MARY JO LEISURE
- ARLENE LINTON

- DEB MALEWSKI
- TONI MCGUIRE
- JAMIE MILLS-PRICE
- JO AVIS MOORE
- TINA SUE NORRIS
- GOLDA RADER
- SHARA REINER
- PEGGY STOGDILL
- BOBBIE TAKASHIMA
- MAXINE THOMAS
- ROSEMARY WEST
- SHIRLEY WILSON
- SHARON MCNAMARA-BLACK

# Table of Contents

# Nature Rejoices

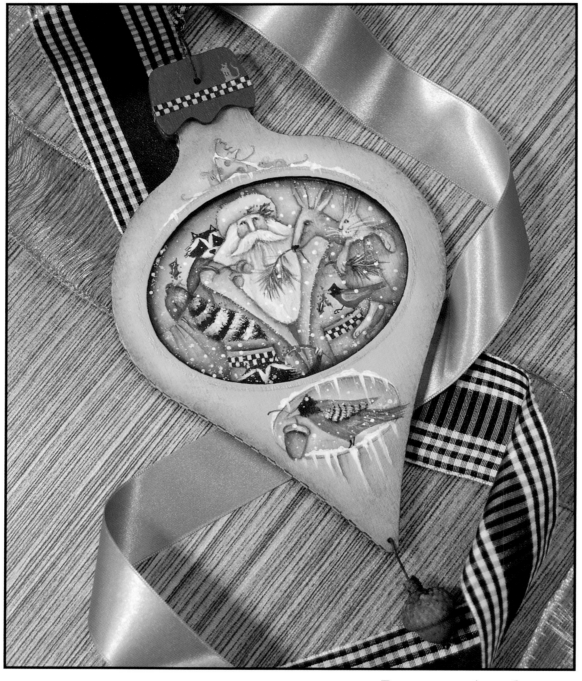

Lynne Andrews

# MATERIALS

*DecoArt Americana Acrylics:* ANTIQUE GOLD • ANTIQUE WHITE • BLUE/GREY MIST • BURNT UMBER • BUTTERMILK • CAMEL • COCOA • DRIED BASIL GREEN • FLESH TONE • HAUSER MEDIUM GREEN • LAMP BLACK • MARIGOLD • PLANTATION PINE • ROOKWOOD RED • SANTA RED • SILVER SAGE GREEN • SNOW WHITE • WILLIAMSBURG BLUE • *DecoArt Dazzling Metallics:* GLORIOUS GOLD

*Loew-Cornell: La Corneille Golden Taklon* 4, 8 ULTRA ROUND, SERIES 7020 • *Maxine's* ¼", ½", ⅜" OVAL MOP, SERIES 270 • 4 SCUMBLER, SERIES 2014 • WHITE NYLON ¼" FLAT GLAZE BRUSH, SERIES 798

DECOART AMERICANA MULTI-PURPOSE SEALER, STAR LITE VARNISH, AMERICANA MATTE ACRYLIC SEALER/FINISHER • ELMER'S GLUE-ALL • KOH-I-NOOR RAPIDOGRAPH PEN, ⁰⁰/.₃₀ BLACK • 400 GRIT SANDPAPER • TRACING PAPER • WHITE AND GRAY TRANSFER PAPER • STYLUS • HAIR DRYER • BLACK AND CREAM CHECK RIBBON • REAL OR WOODEN ACORN AND 2" RUSTY CRAFT WIRE • DRILL AND ¹⁄₁₆" DRILL BIT

# PREPARATION

Base paint the two sections of the ornament with a ³⁄₄" flat glaze brush and one coat of Antique White. Let dry. Lightly sand with 400 grit sandpaper and apply a second coat.

Base paint the cap piece of the of the flat section of the ornament with Rookwood Red. When dry, apply a light wash of Santa Red on top. Base the inside edge of the oval with Lamp Black, and a no. 4 ultra round.

Wash Buttermilk over the front, back, and small oval. Soften with a mop. Dry and repeat.

Transfer the designs to all sections with white transfer paper for the front and gray for the back side.

Apply a light wash of Silver Sage Green to the sky area on all three ovals. Mop to blend and soften.

# TECHNIQUE

Paint the ornament with layers of washes of paint + water. Each layer of wash should be transparent and applied with a no. 4 or no. 8 ultra round. Mop with an appropriate size mop after each layer to blend and soften. Each area will require a minimum of two layers of wash to build up the desired depth of color. Dry completely after each layer of wash to prevent lifting paint.

Detail with a no. 4 ultra round. Stipple with a scumbler.

# STEP 1

Wash Santa's coat with Dried Basil Green, and the hat and coat fur trim with Antique Gold. Wash the top of the hat and section below his beard with Rookwood Red.

Wash the cardinals with Rookwood Red. Let dry. Brighten with a top wash of a Santa Red. Paint the head of the male cardinal Lamp Black.

Wash the deer with Cocoa, the bunny with Camel, and the raccoon's body with Burnt Umber. Fill in the raccoon's mask, ears, and V section between the ears with Lamp Black. Stipple Lamp Black tail bands, followed with Snow White bands.

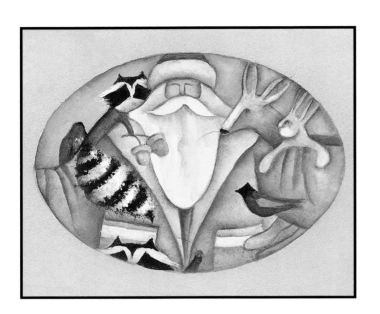

# STEP 3

Add a Marigold beak and a Buttermilk eye dot to each cardinal. Use a pen to make a nostril dot and fill in the legs. Place Plantation Pine holly sprigs with Buttermilk veins and Santa Red berries in each beak.

Paint the raccoons' eyes Buttermilk, and noses Lamp Black. Use either a pen or Buttermilk to establish some hairs around the edges of the faces.

Add strands of Snow White to Santa's hair, beard, and mustache. Outline Santa's eyes and nose with Burnt Umber. Place a dot of Lamp Black and then Buttermilk in each eye. Dry brush the cheeks with Santa Red. Paint the holly on the hat the same as before. Add tiny strokes of Buttermilk to the fur band on the hat and collar.

Free hand Burnt Umber pine branches with Plantation Pine needles. Dot the acorn tips and stroke in bunny whiskers with Buttermilk. Add a Burnt Umber branch with Santa Red berries in the raccoon's paw. Fill in pocket checks with a pen.

# STEP 2

Shade Santa's coat sleeves, under the lapels, and around each pocket with Hauser Medium Green. Dry and reinforce with Burnt Umber. Float Burnt Umber around the beard, mustache, face, hat, and facial features.

Shade the cardinals with Lamp Black. Suggest the male cardinal's wing and the female's breast with Buttermilk.

Shade the raccoon's back with Lamp Black, and the raccoon's tail, deer, acorns, and bunny with Burnt Umber. Highlight the bunny's ears, paws, feet, and cheeks with Buttermilk. Fill in the deer's nose with Lamp Black. Highlight the bridge of the nose with Buttermilk.

Float Burnt Umber around the inside of the oval, on Santa's sleeves and hat, the deer, and the bunny.

# MICE VIGNETTE

Wash the trio of mice at the top of the ornament overlay section with Blue/Grey Mist. Add a touch of Buttermilk if needed.

Define each mouse with a light float of Burnt Umber. Add a dot of Buttermilk for ears and hind legs.

Undercoat the cheese with Buttermilk. When dry, wash with Antique Gold and add Burnt Umber holes in the wedge.

Finish the vignette with Snow White snow on the cheese wedge and along the beveled edge.

# BLUE JAY VIGNETTE

Wash the Blue Jay with Williamsburg Blue. Fill in the head with Lamp Black.

Shade under the wing with Lamp Black. Create wing feathers with alternate choppy strokes of Lamp Black and Buttermilk. Draw the legs with a pen. Add a Marigold eye and beak.

Undercoat the acorn with Buttermilk. When dry, wash Camel on the cap, and Dried Basil Green on the bottom.

Shade between the cap and bottom and down the right side with Burnt Umber. Add a small amount of Lamp Black if needed.

# Ornament top and Back

Base paint the checked band on the separate top piece and back of the ornament with Buttermilk. Draw the checks with a pen, continuing around onto the back. Add a Blue/Grey Mist mouse to the top of the band.

Fill in the lettering with a Rapidograph pen. Dry well and then erase all transfer lines. Paint the mice the same as the front. Add Snow White snow dots, icicles, and sparkles.

Float Burnt Umber + Lamp Black (1:1) under the front and back of the top cap. Float Burnt Umber around the outside edges of the two ornament sections.

# FINISHING

Use a stylus to add dots of Snow White snow all over. When dry, lightly brush on Star Lite Varnish.

Paint Glorious Gold bands around all three ovals. When dry, fill in with Snow White snow and dripping icicles.

Glue the three sections together. Dry thoroughly. Decorate the sides with a checked band, using the pen. Attach a 1" section of rusty wire for hanging and to tie the ribbon to the top.

Drill a small hole through an acorn and at the base of the ornament. Attach the remaining rusty wire through the acorn and ornament and twist to connect the two.

Apply several light coats of sealer to the front, sides, and back of the ornament.

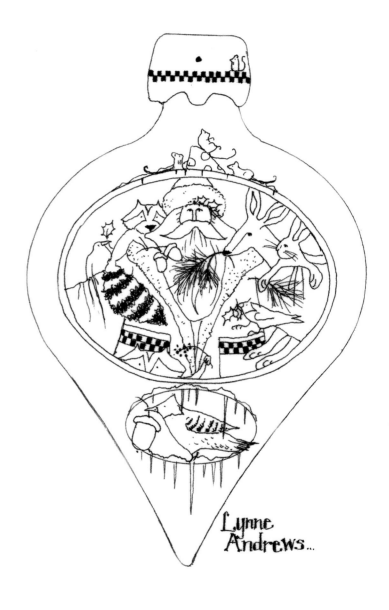

# Old Punkin' Sky

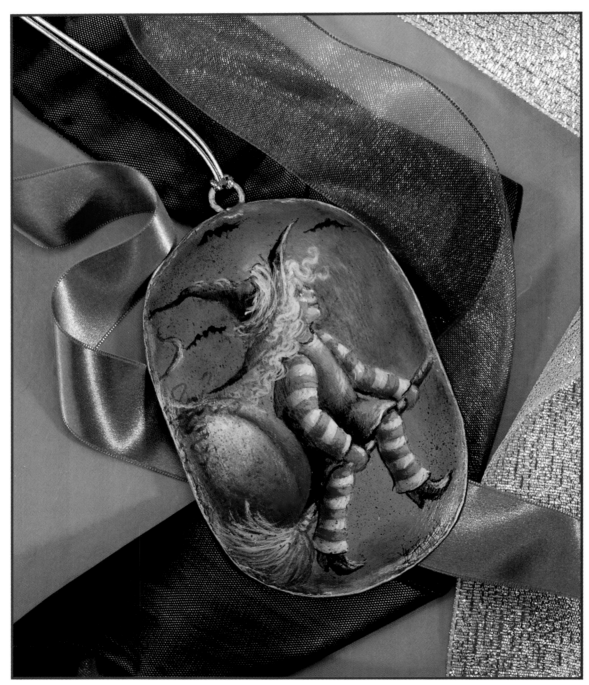

Helan Barrick

# Materials

*Jo Sonja's Artists' Colours:* AQUA • BRILLIANT VIOLET • BROWN EARTH • BURNT SIENNA • CARBON BLACK • GOLD OXIDE • MOSS GREEN • NAPLES YELLOW HUE • NIMBUS GREY • OLIVE GREEN • PALE GOLD • PERMANENT ALIZARINE • RAW SIENNA • SKIN TONE BASE • VERMILLION • WARM WHITE • YELLOW OXIDE • *Jo Sonja's Background Colours:* AZURE • *Jo Sonja's:* RETARDER MEDIUM • CLEAR GLAZE MEDIUM

*Loew-Cornell:* La Corneille Golden Taklon $^{10}$/o LINER, SERIES 7350 • 1, 2 ROUND, SERIES 7000 • 4, 6, 8, 14 SHADER, SERIES 7300 • *Jo Sonja's:* Sure Touch 4, 6 FILBERT, SERIES 1385 • 0, 1 SHORT LINER, SERIES 1360

JO SONJA'S ALL PURPOSE SEALER, SATIN POLYURETHANE VARNISH • TRACING PAPER • STYLUS • WHITE OR GRAY TRANSFER PAPER • WAX COATED PALETTE • PALETTE KNIFE • GOLD CORD • ERASER

# Preparation

Wash the metal ornament in hot, soapy water, then rinse and dry well. Apply a coat of all purpose sealer with a no. 14 shader. Let dry overnight.

Base paint the ornament with Azure. If needed, thin the paint with a little water to promote smooth coverage. Let dry. Apply a second coat and allow to dry.

Transfer the design with gray or white transfer paper.

# Technique

Undercoat each part of the design with smooth, opaque color. Let dry. Apply a light coat of retarder medium with a no. 14 shader. Lightly blot the brush on a paper towel to remove excess fluid before application.

Blend and soften shading on the face and hands with a dry no. 4 filbert and a soft pat-pat stroke. Frequently blot the brush on a paper towel to keep it dry.

Dab shading and highlighting on the clothing with a side loaded shader of appropriate size. Create dabby blending on the pumpkin with a no. 6 filbert. Always dry completely between layers and before proceeding to the next step.

# Step 1

Undercoat the face and hands with one to two coats of Skin Tone Base using a no. 4 shader. Undercoat the clothing and pumpkin with no. 6 and no. 8 shaders. Undercoat the hat, boots, and dress with Carbon Black, and the sleeves and pants with Nimbus Grey. Undercoat the pumpkin with Gold Oxide, the stem with Olive Green, and the broom and handle with Brown Earth.

Transfer interior pattern lines carefully and accurately. Go over pattern lines with a no. $^{10}$/o liner and thinned Burnt Sienna. Let dry. Erase any visible transfer lines.

## STEP 3

Pinken the hands, lips, cheek, tip of nose, and beneath the chin with Vermillion and a no. 1 round. Soften the color with a no. 4 filbert.

Create pants and sleeve stripes with a no. 2 round and thinned Permanent Alizarine. Lighten the front of the hat, dress and shoes with Aqua and a no. 6 shader.

Reshade the pumpkin with Permanent Alizarine + Brown Earth (1:1). Highlight with Vermillion + Yellow Oxide (1:1). Lighten the stem with Moss Green.

Highlight the broom handle and straw with Raw Sienna. Add wispy hair with Brown Earth and a no. 0 short liner.

## STEP 2

Enhance the eye, upper eye line, lash, brow, and mouth line with a no. ¹⁰/₀ liner and Burnt Sienna. Shade the face and hands with Burnt Sienna and a no. 1 round. Soften the color with a no. 4 filbert.

With a no. 6 shader, apply Brilliant Violet to the hat, dress, and shoes. Shade the sleeves and pants with Nimbus Grey + Carbon Black (5:1). Highlight the sleeves and legs with Warm White.

Shade the pumpkin with a no. 6 filbert and Permanent Alizarine. Brighten the broom handle with Raw Sienna and a no. 1 round.

# Step 4

With a no. ¹⁰/₀ liner and Warm White, add a highlight dot in the eye and highlight the cheek, nose, forehead, and chin. Highlight the hair, broom, and handle with a no. 0 short liner and Naples Yellow Hue. Add Burnt Sienna hat band twigs, then highlight the twigs with Naples Yellow Hue. Create Carbon Black bats.

Shade the sleeve and pants stripes with Permanent Alizarine, then highlight with Naples Yellow Hue + Vermillion (3:1). Further lighten the hat, dress, and boots with Aqua + Nimbus Grey + a little Warm White (1:2:1). Lighten the pumpkin with Warm White + Naples Yellow Hue (1:1). Add Burnt Sienna "wisps" around the base of the stem.

After all painting is finished, apply a coat of Clear Glaze Medium to the surface. Let dry. Dampen the surface with a light coat of retarder and blot with a folded paper towel. Pick up a little Pale Gold in the tip of a no. 8 shader and blot on a paper towel. Lightly add soft touches of Pale Gold around the outer edge of the ornament. Dry brush light touches of Pale Gold in the light areas of the pumpkin. Add touches of Pale Gold on the broom straw and twig hat band with a liner.

# Finishing

Seal the ornament with a coat of Clear Glaze Medium. Let dry. Apply two coats of satin varnish with a large shader. When dry, attach a gold cord.

# Forget Me Not

Arlene Linton

# Materials

*Plaid FolkArt Acrylic Colors:* BABY BLUE • BASIL GREEN • LEMON CUSTARD • LIGHT PERIWINKLE • LINEN • MORNING SUN • OLIVE GREEN • THUNDER BLUE •
*FolkArt Artists' Pigments:* YELLOW OCHRE

*Scharff: Kolinski Red Sable* 4 FINE LINE ROUND, SERIES 3000 • MINI FILBERT, SERIES 429

J.W., ETC. FIRST STEP WOOD SEALER • RUST-OLEUM FLAT BLACK SPRAY PAINT • KRYLON GOLD LEAFING PEN • PLAID FOLKART CLEARCOTE MATTE ACRYLIC
SEALER • 400 GRIT SANDPAPER • WHITE TRANSFER PAPER • STYLUS • FACTIS SOFT BLACK ERASER • RICHESON GREY MATTERS PAPER PALETTE • SOFT CLOTH

# Preparation

Seal the ornament with wood sealer. Lightly sand with 400 grit sandpaper. Remove dust with a slightly damp cloth.

Base paint with three coats of Rust-Oleum Flat Black spray paint, allowing the paint to dry between sprays. Dry thoroughly.

Transfer the pattern with white, erasable transfer paper and a fine point stylus. Use an extremely light touch. If needed, remove excess with an eraser. Move and adjust the pattern as you work around the ornament.

# Technique

Paint all the linework, washes, strokes and dots with a no. 4 fine line round brush. Control the consistency of the paint as instructed for each step.

# Step 1

Paint all transferred lines with Linen thinned with water. Hold the brush upright. The inky consistency paint should flow from the fully loaded brush without having to apply pressure.

Test the linework on a piece of dark paper before proceeding to paint on the ornament. When finished, let dry and remove all pattern lines not covered by paint with a black eraser.

Paint a soft wash of Linen in areas designated with the letter W on the pattern. Place a puddle of water on the gray palette and add small amounts of color until the wash is the desired value. The wash should be quite transparent. Let dry. If needed, apply a second or third wash of color to darken.

## STEP 3

Freehand the forget-me-nots with a mini filbert brush.

Undercoat the flowers with Light Periwinkle. Shade with Thunder Blue, and highlight with Baby Blue. Place a Lemon Custard dot in each center. Add a smaller highlight dot of Morning Sun and shade with another smaller dot of Yellow Ochre.

Create leaves with a brush mix of Olive Green and Basil Green. Loosely outline the larger leaves with thinned Basil Green and the flower petals with thinned Baby Blue.

## STEP 2

Freehand fine detail lines with thinned Linen.

*Basic Brush Loading Instructions*
*for Linework and Crosshatching:*

*Carry a couple of brushloads of water to the gray palette. Place a small amount of color on the palette away from the water puddle. Add small amounts of paint to the water with the brush until the mix is the consistency of ink. Use slightly less paint than water in the mix. (Gray palette paper allows the consistency of the paint to be easily visible.)*

*Flatten the brush bristles in the thinned paint. Lift the brush from the puddle. On a clean area of the palette, roll the loaded brush counterclockwise while pulling it up to the brush tip to remove excess moisture.*

# STEP 4

Embellish the linework with strokes and dots of undiluted Linen. Freehand the simple design around the bottom of the ornament with linework, washes, and dots. Refer to the photograph for embellishment placement.

# FINISHING

Protect the ornament with several light sprays of matte acrylic sealer. Gild the ornament cap with a leafing pen.

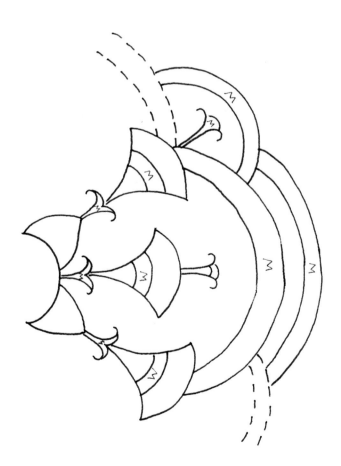

*After the death of Prince Albert in 1861, Queen Victoria was in mourning for the rest of her life. Perhaps these forget-me-nots were a lasting remembrance of the love they shared for twenty-one years.*

# Mr. Santa Claus

Heidi England

# Materials

*Jo Sonja's Background Colours:* CHARCOAL • CHESTNUT • CORNFLOWER • DEEP PLUM • GERANIUM • ISLAND SAND • LINEN • MARIGOLD • RAINDROP • TIGER LILY • WILD GRAPE • WILD ROSE • *Jo Sonja's Artists' Colours:* RICH GOLD • *Jo Sonja's:* CLEAR GLAZE MEDIUM • OPAL DUST

*Jo Sonja's: Sure Touch* 2 ROUND, SERIES 1350 • ¼", ⅜" OVAL GLAZE, SERIES 1390 • 1 SHORT LINER, SERIES 1360 • 2 KOLINSKY LONG POINT ROUND, SERIES 1320

JO SONJA'S ALL PURPOSE SEALER, SATIN POLYURETHANE VARNISH • WHITE TRANSFER PAPER • WHITE PASTEL PENCIL • 400 GRIT SANDPAPER • QUIK WOOD • PALETTE KNIFE • FABRI-TAC ADHESIVE • DECORATIVE YARN AND BEADS

# Preparation

Lightly sand the surface of the ornament. Remove the dust with a damp towel. Apply all purpose sealer with a ⅜" oval glaze brush. Dry.

Base paint the surface with Deep Plum. Let dry.

# Technique

Use paint of a creamy consistency except when washes of paint + water are indicated. Tone, or veil, color with a dirty brush that has one or more colors in the brush at the same time. Add a touch, or tiny touch, of color to the original base color with second, or even, third colors.

# Step 1

Apply the design to the ornament. Sketch the design with just a few pastel pencil lines, or trace and then transfer the design with white transfer paper.

Mold a triangular nose of Quik Wood, following the manufacturer's instructions. Use only about ⅓" of the product. Press onto the face and dry. Paint the nose Deep Plum.

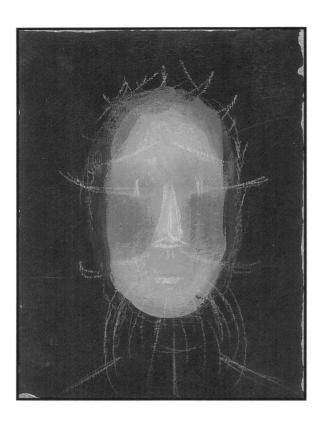

# STEP 3

With a no. 2 long point round, paint the eyes and all the dark lines with Deep Plum + a touch Marigold ($1:\frac{1}{4}$). Darken the pupils with Deep Plum + Cornflower ($1:1$).

Paint the whites of the eyes with Island Sand thinned with water. Highlight the top of the nose, the top of the lower sides of the nose, and the eyelids with creamy Island Sand.

Stroke in the eyebrows, mustache, beard, and pom-pom with a gray mix of Linen + a touch Charcoal ($1:\frac{1}{8}$).

# STEP 2

Undercoat the entire face with a flesh color mix of Island Sand + Marigold + Chestnut ($1:\frac{1}{4}:\frac{1}{4}$) and an oval glaze brush.

Shade the outer edges of the face, under the nose, the fulcrum, and the sides of the nose with flesh color mix + a touch Chestnut. Highlight the forehead and the top of the nose with Island Sand. Wipe the brush. Pick up Wild Rose + a touch Geranium and blush the cheeks.

Add cool blue color in the eye area and across the bridge of the nose with a touch of Cornflower + tiny touch Island Sand.

Sketch, or trace and transfer, the facial features with a white pastel pencil or white transfer paper.

# $S$TEP 4

Dab in the stocking cap and shoulders with an oval glaze brush and Deep Plum + Geranium (1:1), then highlight with Geranium + Wild Rose (1:½).

Highlight the eyebrows, mustache, and beard with a no. 2 round and gray mix + a bit more Island Sand. Add more Island Sand as you highlight. Allow some of the first layers of gray to show. Pounce Island Sand over the hat pom-pom.

Paint the mouth with the Geranium and Wild Rose mix. Add Deep Plum + Cornflower eyelashes. Highlight the eyes and cheeks with Island Sand. Line under the eyes and add laugh lines beside the eyes with Chestnut + a touch Deep Plum (1:⅛).

Add touches of Rich Gold, Wild Grape, and Raindrop around the outer edge. Accent with a little Rich Gold.

# $F$INISHING

Seal the ornament surface with one coat of Clear Glaze Medium. Dry. Apply one coat of satin varnish.

Attach a strand of variegated red yarn around the outer edge with fabric adhesive.

Apply Opal Dust just to the inside of the yarn. Place red and a few aqua beads on the wet Opal Dust. Let dry.

Apply an additional coat of satin varnish.

# Carrot Hugs

Peggy Harris

# MATERIALS

*Jo Sonja's Artists' Colours:* BURNT SIENNA • BURNT UMBER • CADMIUM SCARLET • CADMIUM YELLOW MID • CARBON BLACK • MOSS GREEN • SAP GREEN • TITANIUM WHITE • *Jo Sonja's:* MAGIC MIX • OPAL DUST

*Silver Brush, Ltd.: Golden Natural* 4 FILBERT, SERIES 2003S • *Ruby Satin* 1/8" FILBERT GRASS COMB, SERIES 2528S • 2 BRIGHT, SERIES 2502S • *Ultra Mini* 2 DESIGNER ROUND, SERIES 2431S • 20/0 SCRIPT LINER, SERIES 2407S • 12/0 POINTED ROUND, SERIES 2400S • 12/0 ANGULAR, SERIES 2406S

ELECTRIC HAND SANDER WITH 100 GRIT SANDPAPER • 400 GRIT SANDPAPER • TRACING PAPER • STYLUS • GRAY TRANSFER PAPER • MASTERSON STA-WET PALETTE • NARROW GREEN RIBBON • NEEDLE AND THREAD

# PREPARATION

Reshape the ornamental hanger and the bottom finial to more closely resemble carrots. Use an electric sander and 100 grit sandpaper. Be careful not to sand totally through the porcelain. Lightly sand the reshaped ornament with 400 grit sandpaper to remove marks. Remove sanding dust.

Trace and transfer the design as lightly as possible with a fine-point stylus and gray transfer paper.

# TECHNIQUE

Repeat layers of paint and Magic Mix infinite times to brighten highlights, deepen shading, add color glazes, or add more fluff to fur.

Keep paint and Magic Mix on a wet palette. Magic Mix extends the open time of the paint, then dries to a hard film which may be over painted once dry to the touch.

If instructions do not call for applying Magic Mix over an area before painting, mix a touch of Magic Mix directly into the color to ensure it will dry to a hard film. Always apply Magic Mix to fur areas and areas to be blended before applying paint.

# STEP 1

Dot the eye with a medium-point stylus and Carbon Black. Paint the muzzle and inside the ear with a no. 12/0 angular and Titanium White + a touch Cadmium Scarlet. While wet, lighten the top of the ear with more Titanium White.

Undercoat the carrots with a no. 12/0 angular and Cadmium Yellow Mid + a touch Cadmium Scarlet. Add Moss Green stems with a no. 2 designer round.

# STEP 3

Using the same technique, reapply Magic Mix and begin to deepen the color in some areas with a second layer of soft brown mix. Add some Burnt Umber shading into the darkest areas as you work.

Repeat applications of Magic Mix and paint to gradually improve and refine the fur. Deepen shading and adjust colors gradually, one layer at a time, drying between layers.

With a no. 4 filbert, apply Magic Mix and paint a transparent layer of soft brown mix over rough-looking fur areas. Tint some areas such as the hip and cheek with touches of transparent Burnt Sienna + Magic Mix. Dry.

Shade the carrots with a no. ¹²/₀ angular and Cadmium Scarlet + Cadmium Yellow Mid and/or Burnt Sienna. Highlight with Cadmium Yellow Mid and a pointed round.

Freehand lacy carrot tops with Moss Green and a designer round. Shade with Sap Green + Carbon Black.

# STEP 2

Apply a slick of Magic Mix to fur areas with a filbert grass comb. Wipe the brush and sparsely load with a soft brown mix of Burnt Umber + a touch Cadmium Yellow Mid.

Lay in rows of fur in the direction and angle shown in the photo. Avoid highlight areas of the fur. Wipe the brush clean, and continue to groom the wet fur using extremely short strokes. Blend the edges of the highlights with the same short strokes and a clean brush moistened with Magic Mix.

Add more paint or Magic Mix as desired. Continue stroking as long as the paint remains wet and workable.

Remove paint that strays into unwanted areas with a clean, damp bright eraser brush. It is best to stroke fur through the bottom of the carrot and then remove it with the bright brush, rather than try to paint around the carrot.

Dry the painting thoroughly before proceeding.

# STEP 4

Perfect the Carbon Black eye. Place a sparkling Titanium White highlight on the eye with a ²⁰/₀ liner.

Enhance the muzzle and cheek line with Titanium White and a no. ¹²/₀ angular. Add three tiny Carbon Black whisker dots with liner.

Paint the paws and add a fluffy tail with heavy Titanium White and a pointed round. With a liner dipped in Magic Mix and then Burnt Umber, paint fuzzy toe lines.

Brighten hip and shoulder highlights with a filbert grass comb and a touch Titanium White. Dry the painting thoroughly.

# FINISHING

With a no. 4 filbert, seal the painting with a smooth slick of Magic Mix. Dry thoroughly.

Apply a light coat of Opal Dust to the bunny's carrot. Pick off any larger mica particles. Paint multiple heavier coats of sparkling Opal Dust on the ornament carrots. Let dry.

Gather narrow green ribbon "carrot tops" with a needle and thread. Secure around the bottom finial and ornamental hanger. Add a hanging loop tied with streamers hanging down the back of the ornament.

*Adult bunnies need about 4 cups of veggies every day!*

# Angel Stocking

Shara Reiner

# MATERIALS

*DecoArt Americana Acrylics:* ANTIQUE ROSE • COUNTRY RED • FLESH TONE • FOLIAGE GREEN • HAUSER DARK GREEN • HAUSER MEDIUM GREEN • LAMP BLACK • REINDEER MOSS GREEN • SPICE PINK • SUMMER LILAC • TANGELO ORANGE • TRADITIONAL BURNT SIENNA • TRADITIONAL BURNT UMBER • WARM WHITE • WINTER BLUE

*Scharff: Golden Taklon Champagne Handle* 8, 16 FLAT, SERIES 142 • 8 FILBERT, SERIES 432 • *Golden Taklon* 1 DRESDEN LINER, SERIES 455 • STENCIL BRUSH

DECOART AMERICANA MATTE ACRYLIC SEALER/FINISHER, MULTI-PURPOSE SEALER • CREATIVE COACH SNOWFLAKE STENCIL BCS185 • TRACING PAPER • GRAY TRANSFER PAPER • SANDPAPER • STYLUS • WAX COATED PALETTE • BLACK PERMANENT PEN • WHITE GLUE • $^{1}/_{4}$" BUTTON PLUGS FOR BERRIES • $^{1}/_{8}$" WOODEN HOLLY LEAVES • RUSTY WIRE • SMALL BUTTON

# PREPARATION

Sand and seal the wooden ornament. Base paint the stocking with Reindeer Moss Green. Let dry. Transfer the pattern with gray transfer paper and a stylus.

# TECHNIQUE

Undercoat the basic elements of the design. When dry, shade and highlight the design with floats of color. Accent the design with black penwork as desired.

Select brushes of appropriate size and style for each step as described in the instructions.

# STEP 1

Stencil snowflakes on the stocking with Warm White. Refer to the photograph for placement. For best results, use a stencil brush and a scant amount of paint. Build color gradually.

Undercoat the toe patch and background of the cuff with Winter Blue, and the heel patch and roses on the cuff with Spice Pink.

Undercoat the face with Flesh Tone and the angel wings with Warm White. Shade the wings with Winter Blue next to the face.

## STEP 3

Add whimsical Lamp Black eye dots to the face. Create ros
cheeks with a thin wash of Antique Rose. Deepen the color in th
center of each wash. With a liner, stroke in a nose of Fleshton
+ Burnt Sienna.

Highlight the roses with Warm White and a liner. Stroke i
Hauser Medium Green leaves with a no. 8 filbert. With a liner
add small leaves of Hauser Dark Green.

Highlight the holly leaves with Foliage Green and the berrie
with Spice Pink.

## STEP 2

Shade the top of the face with Fleshtone + Traditional Burnt
Sienna. Line the plaid pattern on the background of the cuff
with Warm White. Shade the roses with Country Red.

Stripe the toe patch on the stocking with Warm White and a no.
8 flat brush. Line a narrow stripe on each side of the wide stripe
with Warm White.

Create a plaid pattern on the heel patch with a wash of Country
Red and a no. 8 flat. Overstroke areas where the plaid crosses to
intensify the color.

Undercoat the holly leaves with Hauser Medium Green. Shade
with Hauser Dark Green. Undercoat the berries with Antique
Rose, and shade with Country Red.

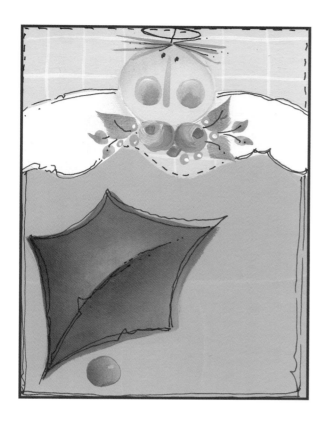

# FINISHING

Glue the cuff to the top of the stocking and the button to the toe patch. Attach the holly leaves to the stocking, and then the berries next to the leaves.

Spray with several coats of sealer/finisher.

# STEP 4

With a liner, stroke Tangelo Orange hair on the angel. Add Summer Lilac filler flowers around the roses. Highlight the flowers with Warm White. Highlight the holly berries with Spice Pink + Warm White.

Create stitch marks in the stocking, double wiggly lines around the stocking and angel wings, a halo, and holly leaf accents with a black permanent pen.

SIZE PATTERN TO FIT SURFACE

# Christmas Roses

Trudy Beard

# MATERIALS

*Plaid FolkArt Acrylic Colors:* CARDINAL RED • FOREST MOSS • MAGENTA • VIOLET PANSY • *FolkArt Artists' Pigments:* BURNT CARMINE • HAUSER GREEN DARK • HAUSER GREEN LIGHT • PURE BLACK • WARM WHITE • *FolkArt Metallic Colors:* INCA GOLD • *FolkArt:* BLENDING GEL MEDIUM • *FolkArt Sparkles:* GOLD

*Royal & Langnickel: Majestic* ⁵⁄₀ SCRIPT LINER, SERIES 4585 • 2, 4, 6, 8, 12 SHADER, SERIES 4150

KRYLON WHITE SPRAY PRIMER • ELMER'S WHITE GLUE • 400 GRIT SANDPAPER • TRACING PAPER • WHITE TRANSFER PAPER • STYLUS • WAX COATED PALETTE • SMALL NATURAL (NOT SMOOTH) SPONGE ROLLER • MATTE VARNISH • ILLUSTRATION BOARD • FINE GOLD METALLIC THREAD • NARROW PINK RIBBONS • TINY BRASS FRAME CHARM • VARIOUS BRASS BEADS • SNOWFLAKE CHARMS

# PREPARATION

Prime and seal the entire sleigh with white spray primer. Dry. Sand with 400 grit sandpaper. Remove sanding dust with a slightly damp paper towel.

Base paint the sleigh with two coats of Forest Moss and a no. 12 shader. Dry between coats. Base paint sleigh runners with Pure Black. Dry. Dry brush over the black with a touch of Inca Gold.

Spread Inca Gold on the palette. Roll a small sponge roller a few times through the paint. Roll once across each side of the sleigh. Dry slightly, then repeat, rolling in the opposite direction. Wash roller immediately.

# TECHNIQUE

Freehand the roses and leaves on the sleigh.

Roughly block-in and shade roses with a small shader. Use Blending Gel Medium to extend the open time of the paint. Use the same brush with no gel to add outer petals and leaves. Add gel to the paint and enhance each rose with transparent outer petals, accents, and highlights.

# STEP 1

Load a no. 4 shader with gel. Blot, then load the same brush with Cardinal Red. Paint the rose shape. Corner load the same brush with Burnt Carmine, then blend on the palette. With the corner loaded with Burnt Carmine pointing toward you, shade the center, right side, and lower edges of the rose shape. Clean the brush. Squeeze dry.

# STEP 3

Stroke in lighter petals with Magenta + a bit more Warm White.

Add more leaves with Hauser Green Light and Hauser Green Light + Warm White. Create additional dark value leaves with Violet Pansy + Hauser Green Dark.

Indicate filler flower buds with a few strokes of Magenta and Violet Pansy.

# STEP 2

Stroke in dark leaves with a no. 4 shader loaded with Hauser Green Dark + a tiny touch Violet Pansy. Clean the brush. Squeeze the brush dry.

Stroke in the first layer of rose petals with Magenta + a small amount of Warm White. Start below the shaded throat of the rose. Pull strokes from each side, and then across the lower edge of the shape. Apply some strokes with light pressure and some strokes with the chisel edge of the brush.

# STEP 4

Add transparent outer petals with gel + Magenta + Warm White. Use more gel than paint to make the paint transparent. Paint petals over the leaves. Adjust the highlights and dark areas with color + gel.

Paint transparent Violet Pansy + Warm White + gel accent color on the dark side, over the leaves. Add Burnt Carmine dots in flower centers, then highlight with tiny Inca Gold dots.

Use a stylus to embellish the side edges of the sleigh with large Inca Gold dots. Dry thoroughly. Paint the inside of the sleigh and the edges with Gold Sparkles paint.

# FINISHING

Create a miniature rose painting on illustration board. Varnish and secure in the frame.

Apply two or more coats of matte varnish to the sleigh. Let dry.

Tie ribbons to each tin scroll on the back of the sleigh. Secure with a tiny bit of white glue.

Attach beads and charms to ribbons. Use fine gold metallic thread to attach charms that have tiny holes. Tie the charms to the pink ribbons and secure the knots with a tiny bit of white glue.

# Three Wise Men

Maxine Thomas

# MATERIALS

*DecoArt Americana Acrylics*: ANTIQUE TEAL • ANTIQUE WHITE • BURNT SIENNA • DARK CHOCOLATE • DEEP MIDNIGHT BLUE • HERITAGE BRICK • HONEY BROWN • KHAKI TAN • LAMP BLACK • LIGHT BUTTERMILK • MARIGOLD • MEDIUM FLESH • MILK CHOCOLATE • NEUTRAL GREY • PRIMARY YELLOW • SOFT BLACK • *DecoArt Hot Shots*: FIERY RED • THERMAL GREEN • *DecoArt Dazzling Metallics*: SPLENDID GOLD • *Weber Professional Permalba Oil Colors*: BURNT UMBER

*Loew-Cornell: La Corneille Golden Taklon* 4 FILBERT, SERIES 7500 • 12 FLAT SHADER, SERIES 7300 • $^{10}/_0$ LINER, SERIES 7350 • *Maxine's* $^3/_8$" MOP, SERIES 270

DECOART AMERICANA MULTI-PURPOSE SEALER, ONE STEP CRACKLE, AMERICANA MATTE ACRYLIC SEALER/FINISHER • FINE GRIT SANDPAPER • TRACING PAPER • WHITE TRANSFER PAPER • STYLUS • WAX COATED PALETTE • ODORLESS THINNER • ALEENE'S TACKY GLUE • 1" RUSTY STAR

# PREPARATION

Sand and use Multi Purpose Sealer to seal both sections of the wooden ornament. Base paint the top section with Honey Brown and then Lamp Black on the cap. Base paint the underlying section with Khaki Tan. Let dry.

To aid in correct pattern placement, place the two sections together and mark the oval picture shape on the lower section. Transfer pattern lines for the town scene at the horizon line.

# TECHNIQUE

Undercoat the basic elements of the design. When dry, shade and highlight the design with floats of color. Gently tap floated color with a mop to soften any harsh lines of color.

Select brushes of appropriate size and style for each step described in the instructions.

# STEP 1

Undercoat the night sky Deep Midnight Blue, and the buildings and trees Lamp Black. Add Marigold windows and Splendid Gold stars. Highlight the building domes and trees with Honey Brown. Let dry and transfer the wise men pattern.

Undercoat the kneeling wise man with Medium Flesh hands and face, Neutral Grey beard, Honey Brown coat, Antique Teal mantle, and Splendid Gold crown and robe details.

Undercoat the bending wise man with Medium Flesh hands and face, Dark Chocolate beard, Antique Teal hatband, Heritage Brick robe, Antique White mantle, and Splendid Gold feathers.

Undercoat the standing wise man with Milk Chocolate hands and face, Soft Black beard, Honey Brown hat, Antique Teal robe, Heritage Brick mantle, and Splendid Gold robe bands.

# STEP 3

Highlight the kneeling wise man's face and hands and create beard and mustache lines with Light Buttermilk. Highlight the crown and robe with Primary Yellow and the mantle with Thermal Green.

Highlight the bending wise man's face and hands, crown of hat, and mantle with Light Buttermilk. Line the beard and mustache with Honey Brown. Highlight the end of the feathers with Primary Yellow, the hat rim with Thermal Green, and the robe with Fiery Red.

Highlight the standing wise man's face and hands and softly line the beard and mustache with Honey Brown. Highlight the hat and gold robe band with Primary Yellow, the robe with Thermal Green, and the mantle with Fiery Red.

# STEP 2

Shade the kneeling wise man's face and hands, crown, and robe with Burnt Sienna. With Soft Black, strengthen the shading behind the arm, above the lap, and down the back. Shade the mantle with Soft Black.

Shade the bending wise man's face and hands with Burnt Sienna. Shade the beard, mustache, and robe with Soft Black, and the mantle with Dark Chocolate.

Shade the standing wise man's face, hands, mantle, and robe with Soft Black, beard and mustache with Lamp Black, and hat with Burnt Sienna. Let dry, then strengthen the shading of the crown of the hat with Soft Black.

# Step 4

Undercoat the gifts Splendid Gold. Shade the gifts with Soft Black and highlight with Primary Yellow. Line the eyes with Lamp Black. Add tiny Light Buttermilk highlights to the bending and standing wise men's eyes.

Decorate the bending wise man's coat with large dots of Soft Black and smaller dots of Splendid Gold.

Decorate the standing wise man's mantle with Splendid Gold stripes. Stripe the hat rim with Heritage Brick. Highlight the center of each stripe with Fiery Red.

# Finishing

Shade the background with Dark Chocolate. Where needed, accent the design with Lamp Black lines. Paint the word "Peace" on the ornament cap with a liner and Splendid Gold. Drag some Spendid Gold over the rusty star.

Coat the top section of the ornament with crackle medium. When dry, antique the section with Burnt Umber oil paint. Dry thoroughly.

Spray all pieces with sealer/finisher. Glue the ornament sections together and attach the star.

# Sweet Santa

Shirley Wilson

# MATERIALS

*Jo Sonja's Artists' Colours:* BRILLIANT GREEN • NORWEGIAN ORANGE • PAYNES GREY • SAPPHIRE • VERMILION • WARM WHITE • *Jo Sonja's Background Colours:* CASHMERE • *Jo Sonja's:* MAGIC MIX

*Jo Sonja's: Sure Touch* ¼", ⅜", ½" POSSIBILITIES, SERIES 1315 • 2 SHORT LINER, SERIES 1360

JO SONJA'S SATIN POLYURETHANE VARNISH • 3M FINE SANDING DISC • TRACING PAPER • 2 PENCIL • HOMEMADE TRANSFER PAPER • STYLUS • WET PALETTE • MINIATURE SPARKLING ICICLES

# PREPARATION

Apply a single light wash of Cashmere to the ornament. Let dry. Sand lightly. Apply the pattern with homemade transfer paper. Omit facial features, leaves, and berries. Take care to avoid an overly dark or heavy-handed transfer.

To make homemade transfer paper: Lightly rub a small piece of tracing paper with a no. 2 pencil. Rub the coating with a small wad of tracing paper to distribute and settle the graphite. This sheet will produce a good transfer with no oily residue.

# TECHNIQUE

Begin the painting loosely with soft undefined edges, most of which should remain out of focus in the finished piece. Use very little paint and keep detail to a minimum. This casual approach allows Santa's smiling eyes and sweet spirit to shine forth.

Use Magic Mix as desired, allowing a brief drying time between applications. Keep a small puddle on a damp palette alongside the paints. Magic Mix may be used to pre-moisten the surface just prior to various paint applications, or sometimes can be simply added to the brush along with the color being used. You will quickly get a feel for using this helpful painting medium.

Select appropriate size Possibilities brushes for most painting. Use a short liner for details. The term "moving to" indicate that it is not necessary to clean the brush between colors. In fact, it is desirable to carry a bit of color as you move to the next color.

# STEP 1

Lightly undercoat the areas of Santa's face, beard, and cap with Magic Mix. Extend the mix somewhat beyond the outer edges of the design.

Thinly undercoat Santa's face and beard with Cashmere. Move to small additions of Sapphire to suggest cool shadows. Lightly place the cap with Vermilion. Let dry.

# STEP 3

Once the surface is completely dry, lightly transfer the remaining pattern lines.

Lightly sketch facial features and the soft shadows that edge the cap with a brown mix of Vermilion + Brilliant Green. Keep the sketch very delicate until you are pleased with the expression. Suggest the mustache and brows with Cashmere + Warm White.

Place the berries and deepen beard and fur shadows with variations of Sapphire + Cashmere.

# STEP 2

Base Santa's face with a delicate flesh tone mix of Cashmere + Vermilion and small touches of Warm White. Move a little of this tone out onto the fur and beard. Keep the edges soft and loose. Allow to dry.

Add slightly stronger Sapphire shadows to the beard and fur and Vermilion accents to the cap. If desired, adjust the face tone with a second application of color.

# STEP 4

Thinly wash the irises of the eyes with Sapphire and paint the eyelashes with Paynes Grey + Vermilion. Move lesser amounts out to accent the mouth and shadows beneath the cap fur.

Place toned lavender shadows of brush mixed Sapphire + Warm White + a touch Norwegian Orange near the eyes and scattered down the right side of the painting.

Deepen facial blushes with Warm White + Vermilion + Norwegian Orange. Strengthen shading on the cap with Norwegian Orange. Deepen the shadows under the berries with Norwegian Orange + Paynes Grey.

Build highlights with Warm White + a touch Cashmere. Move to Warm White in the brightest areas.

# FINISHING

If desired, decorate the back of the ornament with a small Norwegian Orange heart and the inscription, "... On Earth Peace, Goodwill Toward Men".

Finish the ornament with two or more coats of satin varnish.

*Shhh...*

*you may not see or hear him,*
*but when Sweet Santa*
*passes by, spirits lift, eyes*
*shine, and lightheartedness*
*abounds.*

# Pumpkin Moon

Bobbie Takashima

# MATERIALS

*Jo Sonja's Artists' Colours*: AMETHYST • BRILLIANT GREEN • CADMIUM YELLOW LIGHT • CARBON BLACK • PACIFIC BLUE • PURPLE MADDER • SMOKED PEARL • TITANIUM WHITE • YELLOW ORANGE • *Jo Sonja's Background Colours*: TIGER LILY • *Jo Sonja's*: ALL PURPOSE SEALER • CLEAR GLAZE MEDIUM • OPAL DUST

*Jo Sonja's: Sure Touch* ¹/₂" POSSIBILITIES, SERIES 1315 • 10 POINTED ROUND BLENDER, SERIES 2040 • 2 ROUND, SERIES 1350

JO SONJA'S GLOSS POLYURETHANE VARNISH • TRACING PAPER • WHITE TRANSFER PAPER • WAX COATED PALETTE • HOT GLUE GUN • 10" HALLOWEEN FRINGE • 10" GATHERED NETTING • HALLOWEEN RIBBONS

# PREPARATION

Base paint the ornament with a ¹/₂" Possibilities brush and a mix of sealer + Carbon Black. Let dry.

Trace the design on tracing paper. Transfer the pattern with white transfer paper.

# TECHNIQUE

Use a layering technique to build all areas of the design from the darkest value to the lightest, in gradual overlapping layers.

Load an appropriate size brush for the area with a full load of paint + a touch of Clear Glaze Medium. Tap excess paint from the bristle tips before applying the first strokes. This will help to control the amount of paint on the surface.

Begin color application in the center of each round or contoured shape. Stroke gradually to the edges of the round shape to create an illusion of dimension and good form. Use the same procedure for each layer of lighter values.

Allow dark background color to filter through the brush strokes in all the implied shadows to make the shape more believable and to create streaky, "painterly" strokes.

# STEP 1

Undercoat the moon and pumpkins with Purple Madder and a no. 10 pointed round blender.

With the same brush, base the hill Pacific Blue. Begin at the top of the hill and brush color in a gentle curve from side to side, fading the colors from the top curve of the hill to the outer edges and bottom of the ornament shape.

## STEP 3

Base all facial features with a no. 2 round and Carbon Black + a touch Clear Glaze Medium.

Lighten and brighten the moon and pumpkins with Tiger Lily + Yellow Orange (1:1), and the hill with Brilliant Green + Cadmium Yellow Light (1:1). Sketch the witch, dog, clown, and bats with Carbon Black + a touch water and a no. 2 round.

## STEP 2

Begin to gradually lighten and brighten the colors of the moon and pumpkins with a brush mix of Purple Madder + Tiger Lily (1:1) and a no. 10 pointed round blender.

Lighten and brighten the hill with Brilliant Green. Begin at the top of the hill, stroking the brush from side to side in a gentle curve. Allow some background colors to show through.

## FINISHING

Add to the mystique and charm of the pumpkin moon scene with overlapping streaks of "OOhy, BOOy" clouds in Pacific Blue, then Smoked Pearl. With a Possibilities brush, pull the wavy brush strokes from the outer edge of the ornament toward the center. (The spooky strokes work best if you make the eerie sounds as you paint!) Let dry.

Swirl spirals of sparkling Opal Dust over the entire painting. Dry thoroughly. Apply several coats of gloss varnish. For added fun, hot glue embellishments of gathered netting and ball fringe to the bottom edges of the ornament. Use Halloween ribbons to hang the ornament.

## STEP 4

Highlight the moon and pumpkins with Yellow Orange + Cadmium Yellow Light + Titanium White (1:1:1). Accent the sides of the moon and pumpkins with Pacific Blue, then a touch of Amethyst for color interest. Use the same colors along the edges of the moon's eyes and mouth.

Place a tiny stroke of Tiger Lily along the left side of the moon's eyes, and a shine dot of Cadmium Yellow Light + Titanium White (1:1) on the right side. Casually stroke on the moon's eyebrows and hair on the top of the head with Purple Madder.

Lighten and brighten the hill with the last green mix + Cadmium Yellow Light + Titanium White (1:1:2).

Perfect the silhouetted figures and paint the fence with Carbon Black + a touch water and a no. 2 round brush. Scribble shadows with a no. 2 round brush and thinned Carbon Black.

# Elegant Roses

Mary Jo Leisure

# MATERIALS

*Winsor & Newton Artists' Oil Colours:* ALIZARIN CRIMSON • CADMIUM YELLOW PALE • IVORY BLACK • RAW SIENNA • TITANIUM WHITE • YELLOW OCHRE

*Bette Byrd:* 4 SHADER, SERIES 920 • 1 LINER, SERIES 930

KRYLON BLACK SATIN ACRYLIC SPRAY • LIBERTY MATTE FINISH SPRAY • MONA LISA GOLD LEAF • MONA LISA GOLD LEAF ADHESIVE SIZE • VINEGAR • BLUE PAINTER'S TAPE • TRACING PAPER • WHITE TRANSFER PAPER • STYLUS • OIL PALETTE • ODORLESS THINNER

# PREPARATION

Wash the tin ornament with soap and water. Repeat with vinegar and water. Rinse and dry well before painting.

Spray the tin with black satin acrylic spray. When dry, seal with matte finish spray before transferring the pattern and painting.

# TECHNIQUE

Brush mix all color mixes, rather than use a palette knife. Use a dry brush technique to blend colors. Work the brush back and forth on the palette until the desired color and value is achieved.

A plus + sign indicates to stroke back and forth in the colors listed. Colors listed inside parentheses ( ) indicate that they are optional, or to pick up a very small amount of color. Use pressure on the brush when mixing on the palette, as well as when applying the paint, and then lift up the brush and blend lightly.

Roses require a great deal of practice and study, but never be afraid to strike out and experiment. Fear can be your worst enemy. Learn by making mistakes and then correcting them.

# STEP 1

Mask areas for the faux finish background with blue painter's tape. Apply a rough mix of Ivory Black, Cadmium Yellow Pale, and Titanium White to the exposed areas. Dab the paint with a crushed paper towel. If the paint doesn't move, add a little odorless thinner to the towel. Dab until the desired look is achieved. Let dry.

Trim the ornament with gold leaf, following the manufacturer's instructions. Transfer the design with white transfer paper.

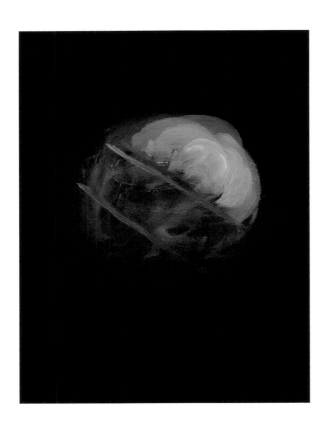

# STEP 3

Add the outside transition, or shadow, petals with the same brus[h] and combination of colors. Begin and end the group of petals a[s] illustrated, midway up the central third section of the fluff ball[.]

Create the central bud, adding more Cadmium Yellow Pale t[o] the mix. The bud should straddle the line marking the centr[al] and upper sections of the fluff ball. Work from the front insid[e] petals toward the outside.

# STEP 2

Stroke in Ivory Black + Raw Sienna + (Titanium White) fluff with a no. 4 shader. Lighten the fluff with (Cadmium Yellow Pale).

Stroke curved petal shapes in the upper third of the fluff ball. Use a combination of Ivory Black, Cadmium Yellow Pale, Yellow Ochre, Raw Sienna, Titanium White, and (Alizarin Crimson) to create light and dark value green mixes.

Paint the back row first, adding as many rows as needed to fill in the area. Work from the outside to the inside.

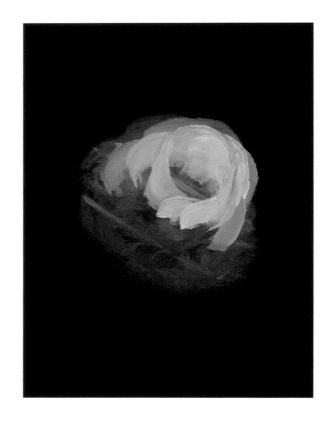

# STEP 4

Complete the bowl with the same brush and color mixes, working from inside to outside. Add the final outside petals to finish the basic form of the rose.

Undercoat the leaves with a green mix of Ivory Black + Cadmium Yellow Pale + (Titanium White). Use a variety of values to establish the position of the leaves.

Spray the wet painting with matte finish spray before proceeding. Let dry thoroughly.

# FINISHING

Enhance the rose with clean darks and lights. Strengthen dark areas with green mixture + Ivory Black + (Alizarin Crimson) (Raw Sienna). Enhance light areas with Titanium White + (Yellow Ochre) + (Cadmium Yellow Pale).

Add tints and accents to create more color in the rose. Tint with Yellow Ochre, light warm green mixes, and (Yellow Ochre + Alizarin Crimson + Titanium White). Accent with Alizarin Crimson + Raw Sienna + (Ivory Black).

Create center dots with a liner brush and Yellow Ochre + (Titanium White).

Shade the leaves with green mixture + Ivory Black + (Alizarin Crimson). Highlight with green mixture + (Cadmium Yellow Pale) + (Titanium White). Wipe the brush and highlight with more Titanium White.

51

# Americana Star

Rosemary West

# MATERIALS

*Jo Sonja's Artists' Colours:* AQUA • BROWN EARTH • CARBON BLACK • NAPTHOL RED LIGHT • ORANGE • PERMANENT ALIZARINE • PINE GREEN • SMOKED PEARL • TITANIUM WHITE • YELLOW DEEP • YELLOW GREEN • *Jo Sonja's Background Colours:* CORNFLOWER • HARBOUR BLUE • MARIGOLD • SHAMROCK • *Jo Sonja's:* ALL PURPOSE SEALER • OPAL DUST

*Silver Brush, Ltd.: Ruby Satin* ³/₈" FILBERT GRASS COMB, SERIES 2528S • 2 FILBERT, SERIES 2503S • *Jo Sonja's: Sure Touch* 3 SHORT LINER, SERIES 1360 • *Royal & Langnickel: Aqualon* 12 FLAT, SERIES 2150

400 GRIT SANDPAPER • TRACING PAPER • WHITE TRANSFER PAPER • WAX COATED PALETTE • OLD STIFF TOOTHBRUSH • ALEENE'S TACKY GLUE • RED AND WHITE SATIN CORD

# PREPARATION

Sand the ornament. Remove sanding dust. Base paint the star with a flat brush and Harbour Blue mixed with all purpose sealer (2:1). When dry, apply a second coat of Harbour Blue.

Dry brush the ornament with Cornflower using a filbert grass comb. Repeat with Aqua + Titanium White (2:1). Begin on the outside of the star using diagonal overlapping strokes. Let dry.

Trace and then transfer the pattern with white transfer paper.

# TECHNIQUE

Paint the ornament using a dry brush technique. Add water to the paint only when doing fine linework. Pick up paint on the tip of the brush. Wipe off just a tiny bit on a paper towel or wax palette. Apply the paint with a light wispy touch. If the paint does not come off the brush with a light touch, pick up more paint, rather than bearing down harder on the brush.

# STEP 1

Dry brush undercoats with a no. 2 filbert in larger areas and a short liner in the smallest areas. Dry brush the eagle's body, wings, and tail with Brown Earth. Begin at the tips of the wings and tail, pulling in toward body.

Dry brush the head with Smoked Pearl, turning the brush on its chisel edge. With the same brush, dry brush the church, house, barn door and roof, and flag.

Dry brush the roofs of the church and house with Cornflower, and the barn, church and house doors, and chimney with Permanent Alizarine.

Base the beak, eye dot, flagpole, cross, and tree trunks with Marigold and a short liner.

# STEP 3

Intensify highlights with a no. 2 filbert. Dry brush the tips of the eagle's wings and tail with Smoked Pearl.

Add lightest highlights on the roofs of the church and house with Aqua + Titanium White. Dry brush Orange on the barn, door of the church and house.

Create details with a short liner. Stripe the flag and paint the heart on the house with Napthol Red Light thinned with a little water. Paint the hayloft, barn door cross braces, house windows and steeple roof lines with Carbon Black. Highlight the beak and paint the eye with Yellow Deep + touch Titanium White.

Highlight the trees with a short liner and streaks of Shamrock.

# STEP 2

Dry brush initial highlights with a no. 2 filbert, or a short liner in smaller areas.

With Brown Earth + Titanium White (1:1) dry brush the eagle. Begin at the front of the breast and the tips of the wings and tail. Leave darker color showing in shaded areas.

Dry brush the eagle's head, house, church, flag, and barn door and roof with Titanium White. Dry brush the roofs of the church and house with Aqua + Titanium White (2:1). With Napthol Red Light, dry brush the barn, doors of the church and house, and chimney bricks.

Base the trees with vertical strokes of Pine Green + a touch Shamrock and a short liner.

# Step 4

Add finishing details with a short liner. Place a tiny Carbon Black pupil dot in the eagle's eye. Thin the paint with water and add dark breast feathers.

Stroke Marigold in the hayloft to resemble straw. Highlight the flagpole, cross, and straw with Yellow Deep + a touch Titanium White. Dab tiny dots of Pine Green and then Shamrock to form the church wreath. Streak highlights on the trees and dab tiny highlight dots on the wreath with Yellow Green. When the wreath is dry, add Napthol Red Light berry dots.

With Titanium White dab snow on the rooftops and trees. Side load the no. 2 filbert with Titanium White and paint chimney smoke and ground snow swirls. Embellish the swirls with tiny dots. Paint the lettering with a short liner. Spatter falling snow with an old stiff toothbrush. Dry.

# Finishing

With an old brush, apply Opal Dust to all areas of the painting except the eagle.

Glue red and white satin cord around the edge of the star. Place glue on one small section at a time and allow to dry before continuing to the next section.

# Tree Toppers

Debbie Cotton

# MATERIALS

*DecoArt Americana Acrylics:* ANTIQUE ROSE • BLACK GREEN • BLACK PLUM • DARK CHOCOLATE • DEEP MIDNIGHT BLUE • FLESH TONE • HAUSER LIGHT GREEN • HAUSER MEDIUM GREEN • HERITAGE BRICK • HONEY BROWN • KHAKI TAN • LAMP BLACK • LIGHT BUTTERMILK • LIGHT CINNAMON • RUSSET • SHADING FLESH • SNOW WHITE • TUSCAN RED • *DecoArt Hot Shots:* FIERY RED • *DecoArt Dazzling Metallics:* SPLENDID GOLD

*Princeton Brushes: Select* 4, 12 FLAT SHADER, SERIES 3750FS • ³/₄" FLAT WASH, SERIES 3750FW • ³/₈" DEERFOOT, SERIES 3750DF • ¹/₄" OVAL MOP, SERIES 3750OM • ³/₈" LUNAR BLENDER SERIES 3750LB • ¹⁸/₀ SHORT LINER, SERIES 3750SL • 2 FILBERT, SERIES 3750FB

DECOART AMERICANA MULTI-PURPOSE SEALER, MATTE ACRYLIC SEALER/FINISHER, WEATHERED WOOD CRACKLING MEDIUM • SPONGE • VINEGAR • SANDPAPER • TRACING PAPER • WHITE TRANSFER PAPER

# PREPARATION

Lightly sand the tin ornament. Do not break the surface of the tin. Wipe the ornament with an equal mix of vinegar and water. Allow to dry. Base paint the surface with equal parts of Multi Purpose Sealer and Khaki Tan. When dry, apply a second coat of this mixture. Dry and repaint with Khaki Tan.

Apply an even coat of crackling medium to both sides of the base-painted tree. When dry, apply a top coat of Black Green with a sponge. Allow to dry and cure.

Shade the outside edges of the tree with Lamp Black using a flat wash brush. Mop to soften. Dry.

Transfer the pattern with white transfer paper.

# STEP 1

Undercoat the face and mouth with a no. 2 filbert and Flesh Tone. Line face details with a no. ¹⁸/₀ short liner and Russet.

Undercoat the hat, coat, and pants with Heritage Brick, mittens with Hauser Medium Green, and boots with Light Cinnamon. Loosely paint the beard with one coat of Dark Chocolate. Stipple Light Buttermilk fur with a ¹/₈" deerfoot.

Allow to dry thoroughly before proceeding.

# STEP 3

Brighten the bottom of the cheeks and nose with Antique Rose. Add Deep Midnight Blue eyes. With a no. 4 flat, shade the beard under the mustache and at the bottom with Dark Chocolate. Deepen with Lamp Black.

Shade the coat and hat with a no. 12 flat shader and Black Plum + Tuscan Red (2:1). Mop to soften. Deepen some areas of the shading with Black Green.

Create a knitted effect on the mittens with a short liner and Black Green lines in shaded areas, and Hauser Light Green lines in highlight areas. Add extra highlights with brush mixed Hauser Light Green + Snow White.

Stipple one coat of Light Buttermilk over fur areas. While the paint is wet, stipple and blend in a small amount of Khaki Tan, then Dark Chocolate.

Shade the boots with Lamp Black. Mop to soften. Add Khaki Tan and Snow White soles with a short liner.

# STEP 2

Shade the face under the hat, at the bottom of the nose and cheeks, and on the top of the inside of the mouth with Shading Flesh using a no. 4 flat. Blend and soften with a ¼" mop.

Brighten the coat, hat, and pants with one coat of Tuscan Red.

Stroke in beard lines with a short liner and Light Buttermilk.

# STEP 4

Dab on eyebrows and highlight the top of the cheeks, beside the pupils, and on the pupils with Light Buttermilk using a short liner. Add Lamp Black eyelids and nostrils.

Stroke in Light Buttermilk mustache and hair lines. Brighten hair and mustache with Snow White top hairs.

Highlight the coat, hat, and pants with Fiery Red. Stipple Snow White highlights on the fur. While wet, pull out tiny hairs with a short liner. Add Lamp Black zigzag lines to the mittens.

Highlight the boot tops with Shading Flesh. With a short liner, add Light Buttermilk highlights to the boot tops and soles. Stroke a fine line of Shading Flesh between the bottom of the boots and the soles.

# FINISHING

Undercoat the star Honey Brown. With a no. 4 flat, shade the bottom of the star and the top of the handle with Dark Chocolate. Deepen handle shading with Lamp Black. Highlight the top of the star with Splendid Gold.

Use a no. 12 flat and Lamp Black to shade the background to the right of Santa. Apply Splendid Gold around the outside edge of the tree with a 3/8" blender. Use the brush in a dry brush fashion but drag it only in one direction.

Spray the ornament with sealer/finisher. Dry.

# The Lamb of God

Jo Sonja Jansen

# MATERIALS

*Jo Sonja's Artists' Colours:* AMETHYST • ANTIQUE GREEN • BRILLIANT VIOLET • BROWN EARTH • CARBON BLACK • CELADON • DIOXAZINE PURPLE • GOLD OXIDE • JAUNE BRILLIANT • NAPTHOL RED LIGHT • ORANGE • PALE GOLD • PURPLE MADDER • RAW SIENNA • RICH GOLD • TEAL GREEN • TITANIUM WHITE • ULTRAMARINE BLUE • YELLOW OXIDE • *Jo Sonja's Background Colours:* MARIGOLD • OAKMOSS • *Jo Sonja's:* RETARDER MEDIUM

*Jo Sonja's: Sure Touch* 3 ROUND, SERIES 1350 • 2 SHORT LINER, SERIES 1360 • ½" SQUARE WASH, SERIES 1375

JO SONJA'S SATIN POLYURETHANE VARNISH • 400 GRIT SANDPAPER • TAPE • TRACING PAPER • WHITE TRANSFER PAPER • STYLUS • WAX COATED PALETTE • PALETTE KNIFE • SMALL CONTAINER FOR MEDIUM • PALETTE COLORS SET UP IN COVERED CONTAINER • SOFT CLOTH

# PREPARATION

Lightly sand the wooden ornament. Remove sanding dust. Base paint the entire ornament with Oakmoss. Dry and sand lightly. Apply a second coat of color if needed.

Trace and then transfer the design to the surface with white transfer paper and a stylus.

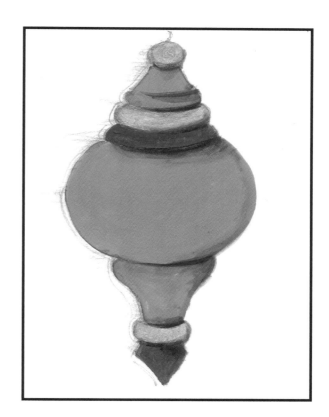

Undercoat the ornament spindles with Rich Gold, Amethyst, and Brilliant Violet as illustrated. Antique or glaze the grooves of the ornament with Dioxazine Purple and a no. 3 round. Use retarder medium to facilitate the blending of color.

Decorate the borders with a no. 2 short liner. Base the scallops with Napthol Red Light. Shade with Purple Madder and highlight with Jaune Brilliant. Add Marigold dots on the Rich Gold border, and Rich Gold stripes on the Brilliant Violet border. Embellish the Amethyst border with Rich Gold dots, Teal Green + Yellow Oxide comma strokes, and Marigold + Titanium White flower dots.

# TECHNIQUE

For longer blending time, blend color with a no. 3 round brush over a very thick application of retarder medium.

Stroke blend the garments and dabby blend the faces and lamb. Stroke borders and details with a no. 2 short liner.

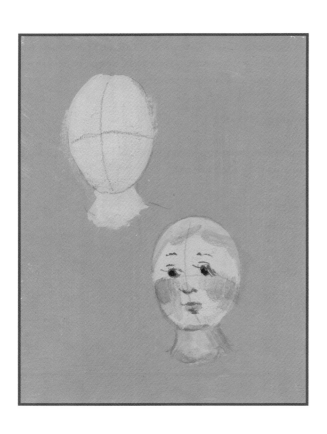

# STEP 2

Shade the faces with Antique Green, moving to touches of Brilliant Violet and Brown Earth. Highlight with Titanium White. Use more Titanium White for additional contrast.

Add a touch of Dioxazine Purple to the dark shadows on the face of the wise man from Africa. Highlight with Jaune Brilliant.

Begin the beards, mustaches, and eyebrows of the European wise man and the shepherds with liner strokes of Raw Sienna followed by strokes of Brown Earth.

Begin the beards, mustaches, and hair of the Asian and African wise men with liner strokes of Brown Earth and darker strokes of Carbon Black. Highlight with Antique Green.

# STEP 1

Undercoat all skin areas with a basic flesh mix of Titanium White + Gold Oxide. Reserve this mix on the wet palette for touch-ups.

Add Brown Earth eyes with Carbon Black pupils. Line with Brown Earth + Carbon Black.

Blush cheeks, tip of nose, under edge of chin, and shadows of the Christ Child's hand with Orange + a touch Napthol Red Light.

# THREE WISE MEN

Paint white garments in the same manner as the Christ Child's gown. Gently stroke blend Purple Madder for the Asian wise man's robe and Ultramarine Blue for the African wise man's robe. Allow the background to show through as the main color.

Paint decorative touches on the garments of the wise men. Under paint the crowns with transparent Marigold. Decorate with Rich Gold. Shade with Purple Madder or Dioxazine Purple, and highlight with touches of Pale Gold. Add a touch of Napthol Red Light on the crown band of the African wise man.

# MOTHER & CHILD

Base Mary's cap and the Christ Child's gown with transparent Titanium White + water. Dry.

Apply a light coat of retarder medium to the surface and shade with Antique Green, moving to Brilliant Violet with touches of Ultramarine Blue and Brown Earth. Highlight with gentle stroke blending of Titanium White.

Softly base Mary's veil with Antique Green. Shade with Ultramarine Blue + a touch Brown Earth. Highlight the veil with Celadon + Titanium White.

Base the Christ Child's hair with Yellow Oxide. Shade with dabby Brown Earth. Highlight with Yellow Oxide + Titanium White.

Delicately under paint the halo areas with transparent Marigold. Decorate with Rich Gold. Shade with Purple Madder or Dioxazine Purple. Highlight with Pale Gold touches.

# SHEPHERD BOYS

Base the right shepherd boy's head covering with Antique Green. Shade with Ultramarine Blue + a touch Brown Earth. Highlight with Celadon + Titanium White.

Base the left shepherd boy's head covering with Marigold. Shade with Gold Oxide, moving to Brown Earth + Purple Madder. Highlight with Marigold + a tiny touch Titanium White.

Gently stroke blend the remaining garments of the right shepherd boy with Marigold, and the left shepherd boy with Purple Madder. Use the background as the main color.

# SHEPHERD & LAMB

Base the shepherd's head covering with Marigold. Shade with Gold Oxide, moving to Brown Earth + Purple Madder. Highlight with Marigold + a tiny touch Titanium White.

Gently stroke blend the remaining garments with Brown Earth, using the background as the main color.

Base the lamb with dabs of transparent Titanium White + water. Dry. Apply a light coat of retarder medium to the surface. Shade with Antique Green, moving to Brilliant Violet with touches of Ultramarine Blue and Brown Earth. Highlight the lamb with Titanium White.

# FINISHING

Dry the painting well. Apply a light coat of retarder medium to the middle painting surface. Gently shade the background with a dabby blend of Teal Green. Carry the color gently down into the garments.

If desired, touch face and garment highlights with a very gentle blush of Rich Gold.

Freehand lettering with a no. 2 short liner and Teal Green + touches of Purple Madder.

Finish the ornament with three or four coats of satin varnish.

ADJUST PATTERN AS NEEDED TO FIT ORNAMENT

# Holiday Poinsettia

Margot Clark

# MATERIALS

*Koh-I-Noor:* RAPIDOGRAPH PENS 0, 1 FILLED WITH *Tranz-Mix Media* BLACK WATERPROOF INDIA INK • PEN CLEANER • OLD ³/₈" ANGLE SHADER

*Margot's:* MIRACLE BRUSH • MIRACLE TEXTURE PAINTING PASTE • *PME* 1 DECORATOR TIP • *Wilton:* 6" DISPOSABLE PLASTIC PASTRY BAG • COUPLER RING SET • RUBBER BAND • PLASTIC SANDWICH BOX WITH WET KITCHEN SPONGE

KRYLON MATTE FINISH SPRAY 1311 • E6000 GLUE • FINE SANDPAPER • TRACING PAPER • WAX-FREE OLD GRAY GRAPHITE PAPER • FINE POINT STYLUS • PALETTE KNIFE • SCISSORS • TOOTHPICKS • LONG PEARL TOPPED PIN • PEARL BEADED TRIM • WHITE HALF PEARLS • TWO SIZES PEARL TEARDROPS

# PREPARATION

Sand the ornament with fine sandpaper to remove any marks. Remove dust with a damp paper towel.

Trace the design onto small pieces of tracing paper for ease of placement on the ornament.

# TECHNIQUE

Delicate ink and texture paste detailing allows the beauty of the porcelain bisque ornament to show through the design. Embellish the black and off-white ornament with pearls and beaded trim.

# STEP 1

Position roughly one half of the design on one section of the ornament. Place gray graphite paper, transfer side down, under the design and lightly transfer the design to the surface with a stylus.

Repeat the transfer on all four sides of the ornament, varying the position of the design. If desired, position so that two sides meet at a corner.

With a no. 0 Rapidograph pen, draw over the pattern lines with ink. Add leaf detail and center berries. Allow to dry thoroughly.

# STEP 3

Prepare the Miracle Mud and pastry bag as instructed.

Apply a bead of paste to a poinsettia leaf. Begin at the tip of the leaf, exert pressure on the pastry bag, and outline one side of the leaf about halfway down the leaf. Return to the tip of the leaf and repeat the process on the opposite side. While the paste is wet, immediately proceed to Step 4.

# STEP 2

Ink the dot shading with a no. 1 Rapidograph pen. Place dots where one design element rests over another. Let one section dry before proceeding to the next. Allow all sides to dry thoroughly.

With a ³/₈" angle shader, apply black India ink to the top, bottom, and side edges of the ornament. Repeat as needed to obtain solid coverage. Allow to dry thoroughly before beginning texture painting.

# Step 4

Dampen the Miracle Brush in water and squeeze out the excess moisture. Flatten the brush slightly, position just under the line of paste, and push up gently into the paste. Pull the brush down toward the calyx, creating one side at a time.

Work quickly to create petals before the paste begins to set up. Do not go back into the paste if it does happen to set up. Add flower centers with quick squeezes of the pastry tip. Allow the paste to dry overnight.

# Finishing

Protect all of the painted, inked, and texture painted surfaces with two light coats of matte finish spray.

Sew pearl teardrops behind the beaded trim. Glue the trim around the bottom and top of the ornament. Fashion a hanger from the long pearl topped pin and glue in place.

*Texture Painting: Preparation*

*Drop inner coupler into pastry bag and position firmly. Trim off excess bag from front of coupler area. Place tip at end of coupler and screw on top coupler. Fold the bag sides down. Fill tip and bag with approximately four tablespoons of Miracle Mud. Roll bag up, twist to force paste into tip until it begins to extrude. Attach rubber band to hold paste down. Trim off excess bag to about 1".*

*Note: When not using bag, stick tip into wet sponge in sandwich box. Clean off the tip with a wet paper towel when necessary. Store tube in lidded box so paste in tip does not dry out. Pastry tube will remain ready to use for a couple of weeks.*

# A Cardinal Gift

Sharon McNamara-Black

# Materials

*Jo Sonja's Artists' Colours:* BLUE VIOLET • BROWN MADDER • COBALT BLUE HUE • MOSS GREEN • NAPTHOL RED LIGHT • ORANGE • RAW SIENNA • RAW UMBER • TITANIUM WHITE • *Jo Sonja's:* ALL PURPOSE SEALER • RETARDER MEDIUM • FLOW MEDIUM • MAGIC MIX • CLEAR GLAZE MEDIUM

*Dynasty: Black Gold* 4 SHADER, SERIES 206S • ³/₈" ANGULAR WAVE, SERIES 206WA • 4 FILBERT WAVE, SERIES 206WFIL • 4 WAVE, SERIES 206WV • ³/₄" FLAT WASH, SERIES 206FW • *Dynasty SC* 4 RIGGER, SERIES 406 • 8 FILBERT, SERIES 416 • LONG POINT LINER, SERIES 418

JO SONJA'S SATIN POLYURETHANE VARNISH • TRACING PAPER • GRAY TRANSFER PAPER • STYLUS • ERASER • WAX COATED PALETTE • PALETTE KNIFE • SCUFFING PAD • ADHESIVE • LEMON-FREE DETERGENT • VINEGAR • HAIR DRYER • 6" 2MM CORDING • SILK TASSEL

# Preparation

Wash ornament with detergent and water. Rinse with vinegar and water. Dry well and apply all purpose sealer. Base paint front of heart with pale blue/green + sealer (3:1). Base paint back with Napthol Red Light + sealer (3:1). Dry well. Scuff the surface and repeat. Trace and transfer the design.

Prepare the color mixes listed next to the pattern.

# Technique

Highlighting and shading snow: Apply a thin coat of retarder medium with a flat wash brush. Sideload no. 8 filbert brush with color, work on dry palette to remove excess moisture, then apply paint. Dry. Seal with Clear Glaze Medium.

Highlighting and shading: Dress brush with Magic Mix, work on palette to remove excess medium, load or sideload with color, work again on dry palette, then apply paint.

Line work: Thin the paint to the consistency of skim milk with flow medium.

Stippling: Dress wave brush with Magic Mix, work on palette, load with color and work again, then gently tap bristles onto the painting surface.

Force drying: Waft warm air over paint and mediums with a hair dryer for faster drying.

Brush selection: Choose the size and style brush that best fits the area in which you are working.

# Step 1

Undercoat design elements. Dress the brush with Clear Glaze Medium, load with paint, work on the palette, and then apply paint. Repeat until the color is opaque. Several thin coats will dry quickly. When finished, erase all visible transfer lines except for snow lines.

Cobalt Blue Hue: sky, shadows below tree, house, and barn
Napthol Red Light: barn front and male cardinal
Pale orange: barn left side, beaks, and feet
Light cream: house left side
Pale green: house front, seed in male's beak, and female cardinal

Cream: house roof shadow on left and house extension on right
Gray: roofs and left sides of chimneys
Light blue: barn right roof and door trim, snow on branch, house left roof edge and windows
Dark blue: barn roof front edge and windows, house roof lower edge and right side of chimneys, cardinals' masks, beak divisions, and eyes
Light brown + touch Titanium White: house door and left side extension shadow
Light brown: house front windows
Dark green: fir trees stippled with no. 4 flat wave
Medium green: branch needles stippled with no. 4 flat wave

Use a filbert wave to stipple Brown Madder shading on mal  cardinal; repeat with Raw Umber. Stipple Moss Green, the  medium green shading on female. Highlight left side of fir tree  medium green, then Moss Green. Shade branch needles an  berry with dark green.

Dry, then apply a barrier coat of Clear Glaze Medium. Pain  snow on branch, barn, and house roofs Titanium White. Shad  lower edge of house front and extension Moss Green, and lef  side of house cream. Apply retarder medium to snow areas an  highlight Titanium White. Let dry. Apply Clear Glaze Medium.

# STEP 2

Shade snow area with a no. 8 filbert sideloaded with light blue; repeat with medium blue. Sideload long edge of angular wave with same colors and shade outer edges of path and road with horizontal streaks. Shade below buildings and fir trees, and on darkest areas on left of road with gray. Shade left side of house extension with dark blue, and snow area on lower right edges of roofs and on right side of fir trees with light blue.

Indicate board separation lines with Raw Umber on barn front, then line shadows on barn door trim, house door, and blue windows. Paint board separation lines on barn side and shade beaks with Orange, then Napthol Red Light. Shade lower edge of barn front Brown Madder.

# STEP 3

Apply retarder medium to sky and wash diagonally with ligh  blue. Paint deciduous trees and line bird's feet with ligh  brown. Paint upper tree branches and flick snowflakes with thi  Titanium White.

Stipple Orange highlights on male cardinal, and use liner to pain  feathers on the female. Shade Orange feathers with Napthol Rec  Light. Highlight female with pale green, then Titanium White  Stipple Moss Green highlights on branch needles.

# Step 4

Highlight male cardinal with light orange, then light cream. With light blue, line lower edges of barn roof and bird eyes and add reflective highlights on male. Paint chimney smoke, highlight chimneys and beaks, and place dots in eyes with Titanium White. Underline female cardinal's tail and wing feathers, base of tail, and cheek with dark gray.

# Finishing

Seal the ornament with Clear Glaze Medium. Allow surface to dry for one week. Apply several coats of satin varnish + water (1:1) to both sides with a soft brush. Attach a tassel to the ornament with adhesive and tie cording through the loop.

## Color Mixes

PALE BLUE/GREEN BASE PAINT =

WHITE + TCH BLUE VIOLET + TCH MOSS GREEN

PALE GREEN = WHITE + MOSS GREEN (3:1)

MED. GREEN = COBALT BLUE HUE + MOSS GREEN (1:1)

DARK GREEN = MOSS + BLUE VIOLET (1:1)

LIGHT CREAM = WHITE + RAW SIENNA (3:1)

CREAM = LIGHT CREAM MIX + RAW SIENNA (1:1)

LIGHT BLUE = WHITE + TCH BLUE VIOLET

MED. BLUE = LIGHT BLUE MIX + TCH BLUE VIOLET

DARK BLUE = BLUE VIOLET + RAW UMBER (1:1)

PALE ORANGE = WHITE + ORANGE (3:1)

GRAY = RAW UMBER + WHITE + BLUE VIOLET (3:2:1)

LIGHT BROWN = WHITE + RAW UMBER (2:1)

# My Little Pretty

Golda Rader

# MATERIALS

*DecoArt Traditions Artist Acrylics*: BURNT SIENNA • BURNT UMBER • CARBON BLACK • CERULEAN BLUE • NAPTHOL RED LIGHT • RAW SIENNA • TITANIUM WHITE • *DecoArt Traditions:* EXTENDER AND BLENDING MEDIUM

*DecoArt Traditions:* 0 MINI MOP • $^3/_0$ LINER • 6 FLAT • $^1/_4$" ANGLE

ACTIVA ACTIV-WIRE MESH • DECOART TEXTURE CRACKLE • PAPER PACKING TAPE • TRACING PAPER • GRAY TRANSFER PAPER • STYLUS • HOT GLUE GUN • BLACK PLASTIC SPIDERS • PALETTE KNIFE • ASSORTED RIBBONS

# PREPARATION

Trace the pattern onto tracing paper. Position the pattern on the ornament. Transfer the pattern to the ornament with a stylus and gray transfer paper.

# TECHNIQUE

In all steps, brush mix the paint with extender and blending medium. Do not clean the brush with water. Rather, just wipe the brush on a paper towel to remove excess paint before proceeding. Use a mini mop to soften shading and highlighting.

# STEP 1

Establish the pattern with a no. $^3/_0$ liner and inky consistency Burnt Sienna + extender and blending medium. Dry.

Base coat the entire ornament with a no. 6 flat brush and a flesh tone mix of Titanium White + Burnt Sienna + Raw Sienna.

# STEPS 2 & 3

Shade all folds and wrinkles with an angle brush and flesh tone mix + Burnt Sienna. Mop to soften.

Highlight the folds and wrinkles with flesh tone mix + Titanium White. Basecoat the eyeballs with Titanium White,

# TEP 4

Add Carbon Black pupils and Cerulean Blue irises with a liner brush. Shade whites of the eyes with Cerulean Blue and an angle brush. With a liner, place a Titanium White reflective light dot in the upper right of pupils. Stroke in eyelashes and eyebrows of inky consistency Carbon Black + Burnt Umber. Add Cerulean Blue highlights at the tips.

Blush the cheeks with flesh tone mix + a touch Napthol Red Light and a flat brush. Mop to blend. Line mole hairs with inky consistency Carbon Black. Add Cerulean Blue highlights.

Undercoat the hair with Burnt Sienna + Carbon Black. Separate sections of hair with a liner and inky consistency Carbon Black. Dry brush some Cerulean Blue highlights in each section.

# FINISHING

Form a witch's hat from Activ-Wire Mesh. Cover the mesh with paper packing tape. Apply texture crackle with a palette knife. Let dry.

Base paint the hat with Cerulean Blue. Antique the hat with Carbon Black. Attach ribbons and spiders to hat with hot glue. Adhere hat to ornament with hot glue, leaving a hole in the hat for a hanger.

*Double, double*
*toil and trouble;*
*Fire burn,*
*and caldron bubble.*

# Hidden Violets

Peggy Stogdill

# MATERIALS

*Winsor & Newton Artists' Oil Colours:* BISMUTH YELLOW • FRENCH ULTRAMARINE • IVORY BLACK • OLIVE GREEN • PERMANENT ALIZARIN CRIMSON • SAP GREEN • TITANIUM WHITE • WINSOR VIOLET (DIOXAZINE) • *DecoArt Americana Acrylics:* LAMP BLACK

*Cheri Rol:* 0, 2, 4, 6, 8 BLENDER • 12 SOFT SYNTHETIC FLAT OR FILBERT • FINE LINER

MONA LISA VARIEGATED BLACK COMPOSITION GOLD LEAF • MONA LISA GOLD LEAF ADHESIVE SIZE • J.W., ETC. RIGHT-STEP SATIN VARNISH • TRACING PAPER • GRAY TRANSFER PAPER • STYLUS • FINE-LINE MARKER • WAX COATED PALETTE • COTTON SWABS • MEDIUM GRAIN SMALL SEA SPONGE • SOFT LINT FREE CLOTH • ODORLESS THINNER • E-6000 GLUE • 3 SMALL FLAT-BACK CRYSTALS • LILAC ORGANZA RIBBON

# PREPARATION

Base paint the top and bottom finials, the ornament back, and the adjoining first ¼" of the side with Lamp Black acrylic and a no. 12 flat or filbert. Leave the front and rest of the side unpainted. Dry and apply a second coat. Let dry. Varnish all black areas with satin varnish.

Transfer the design to the unpainted front and side with gray transfer paper and a stylus.

# TECHNIQUE

Brush mix colors with the approximate ratios indicated. Select blenders of appropriate size for the painting area. Apply pressure to the brush when applying paint. When blending, use as little pressure and as large a brush as possible for the area.

Undercoat a petal or leaf with a small amount of paint. Stretch the paint to just cover the highlight areas. Apply and blend shading, highlights, and tints over the undercoat. Use a dirty brush of paint for tints. Apply highlights with more paint.

In general, apply shading wherever a petal or leaf rolls back away from the light source and apply highlights where they reach up toward the light source.

# STEP 1

Undercoat visible tops of lower three violet petals with Sap Green + Bismuth Yellow + Titanium White (1:1:1). Undercoat remaining petal areas of the blue/violet petals with Winsor Violet + Permanent Alizarin Crimson + Titanium White (4:3:6).

Use Winsor Violet + Permanent Alizarin Crimson + Titanium White (2:3:6) for the red/violet petals. Add more white mix for flipped edges. "Scizzle" back and forth with the chisel edge of the brush to blend the two colors and to create short streaks where they join.

Undercoat background leaves with a blue/green mix of Sap Green + French Ultramarine + Titanium White (1:1:3). Undercoat the foreground leaves with a yellow/green mix of Sap Green + Olive Green (1:1).

Undercoat calyxes, bracts, and grass with Olive Green. Use Sap Green + Olive Green (1:1) for blades at top left. Add a touch of Bismuth Yellow for blades at top center and top right.

# STEP 3

Highlight flowers, leaves, calyxes, and bracts with Titanium White. Use the largest brush possible for each area.

Lift out center veins and delicate side veins on the wet leaves with a small, dry flat brush with a sharp chisel edge.

Create the background around the design with varying ratio of Ivory Black + Sap Green. Extend the color over the edges to meet the black acrylic basecoat on the side. Use as large a brush as possible for each area. Vary the amount of paint used so the color is nearly transparent at times. Slip-slap blend so the brush strokes are still visible.

# STEP 2

Shade tops of upper petals with Winsor Violet + Ivory Black + French Ultramarine (2:1:1). Shade a few petal edges to create form. Blend. With the chisel edge of a brush and a bit of shade mix, sketch short vein lines radiating out from the green petal areas.

Paint and blend subtle tints on some petal edges. Use Permanent Alizarin Crimson on red/violet violets and Winsor Violet + Permanent Alizarin Crimson (1:1) on blue/violet violets.

Shade grass, bracts, and calyxes with Olive Green. Shade leaves at the base of each leaf and a short way up the center. Use Olive Green to shade the foreground leaves and Ivory Black to shade the background leaves.

Place and blend tints of flower color in a wide application on foreground leaves. Use a light flower mix for tints in light leaf areas and a dark flower mix for tints in dark areas.

# STEP 4

With the corner of the no. 0 blender, dab tiny bits of Titanium White onto green areas of the flowers.

Paint stems with Olive Green or Olive Green + a bit of Titanium White and a liner. Highlight with Titanium White. When needed, thin the paint slightly with odorless thinner. Allow the painting to dry completely.

Apply gold leaf size with a dry sea sponge to all black acrylic painted portions of the ornament. Pour some size onto the waxed palette. Lightly tap sponge into the size, tap on a dry area to remove excess, and then tap onto the ornament. Extend lightly into the painted background. Keep it loose and lacy.

Allow the size to tack and apply gold leaf. Dry overnight, then gently rub away excess leaf with a lint-free cloth. Repeat the process in areas that need patching.

# FINISHING

Apply adhesive size to both finials. Allow to tack. Apply small pieces of leaf, overlapping the pieces. Press the leaf into the size by pushing gently with a brush and/or a piece of the rouge paper packaged with the leaf. Dry overnight.

Varnish the entire ornament with satin varnish. Glue tiny crystal "dewdrops" onto the design. Use the ribbon to hang.

# Uncle Sam

Heidi England

# Materials

Jo Sonja's Background Colours: BLACKBERRY • CHARCOAL • CHESTNUT • CORNFLOWER • DEEP PLUM • GERANIUM • HARBOUR BLUE • ISLAND SAND • LINEN • MARIGOLD • RAINDROP • TIGER LILY • WILD ROSE • *Jo Sonja's Artists' Colours:* RICH GOLD • *Jo Sonja's:* CLEAR GLAZE MEDIUM • GOLD DUST • OPAL DUST

*Jo Sonja's: Sure Touch* 2 FILBERT, SERIES 1385 • 2, 6 FLAT, SERIES 1370 • ¼" OVAL GLAZE, SERIES 1390 • 1 SHORT LINER, SERIES 1360.

JO SONJA'S SATIN POLYURETHANE VARNISH • WHITE TRANSFER PAPER • TRACING PAPER • STYLUS • PASTEL PENCIL • FABRI-TAC ADHESIVE • QUIK WOOD • DECORATIVE YARN AND BEADS

# Preparation

Base paint the background Blackberry. Add a tiny bit of Rich Gold around the outer edges. Let dry. Transfer the pattern lines with white transfer paper.

Use a ¼" of Quik Wood to mold a triangular nose, following the manufacturer's directions. Press the nose onto the face. Let Dry.

# Technique

Use paint of a creamy consistency except when washes of paint + water are indicated. Tone, or veil, the color with a dirty brush that has one or more colors in the brush at the same time. Add a touch or tiny touch of color to the original base color with second, or even third, colors.

# Step 1

With a no. 6 flat, undercoat the face and hands with a flesh color mix of Island Sand + touch Marigold + tiny touch Chestnut (1:½:¼). Shade with a little Chestnut. Undercoat the top of the hat with Linen and the hat band and brim with Harbour Blue.

Use a no. 2 filbert to undercoat the shirt with a grayish blue mix of Linen + a touch of Raindrop and Chestnut (1:¼:¼). Paint the bow tie with Geranium. Highlight with Tiger Lily and shade with Deep Plum. Undercoat the hair with a medium gray mix of Linen + Charcoal (2:1).

Sketch or transfer the beard and other pattern lines.

# STEP 3

Add cool color touches of Raindrop + Cornflower in the ey
area and to lower left side of face. Create facial lines, includin
the iris area, nostrils, and eyebrows with a no. 1 short liner an
Deep Plum + Chestnut (1:1).

Tint the cheeks and paint the eyes with an oval glaze brush and
wash of Wild Rose + Geranium + Tiger Lily (1:¹/₂:¹/₂). Add Dee
Plum + Harbour Blue (1:1) pupils and eyelashes with a sho
liner. Shade the sides of the face, under the nose, and under th
hat with an oval glaze brush and a wash of Chestnut + a touc
Harbour Blue (1:¹/₄).

Highlight the hat band, face, eyebrows, beard, and hair wit
Island Sand. Add Island Sand stars to the hat band. Accent wit
Geranium. Stripe the hat with a good no. 2 flat and Geranium

# STEP 2

With a no. 6 flat, undercoat the white part of the flag with Linen.

Paint the jacket and the blue of the flag with Harbour Blue.
Leave a negative space (indicated with pastel pencil lines in the
photo) between the jacket and the jacket shoulder seams, down
the jacket front, and at the lower edge of the sleeve.

Dry brush the background with Geranium + Wild Rose (2:1.)

## FINISHING

Seal the painting with Clear Glaze Medium. Dry.

Glue yarn to the outer edge with Fabri-Tac adhesive that is invisible when dry. Embellish the edges with Gold Dust and Opal Dust just to the inside of the yarn. While wet, drop decorative red, white, and blue beads into the area. Dry.

Protect the ornament with two coats of satin varnish.

## STEP 4

ccent the lower part of the hand with Raindrop. Add a Deep 'lum + Chestnut (1:1) line on the hand.

tripe the flag with the chisel edge of a no. 2 flat and Geranium. reehand Linen stars on the blue field of the flag. Add a skimpy ne of Rich Gold around the flag.

ine the jacket and shirt with Deep Plum + Harbour Blue (1:1). .dd a jacket button of Rich Gold. Flyspeck the outer edges of he ornament with Rich Gold.

# Snow Days

Deb Malewski

# MATERIALS

*DecoArt Americana Acrylics:* ADMIRAL BLUE • BABY BLUE • BITTERSWEET CHOCOLATE • BLACK PLUM • COUNTRY RED • FRENCH VANILLA • GOLDEN STRAW • HAUSER DARK GREEN • HAUSER MEDIUM GREEN • HONEY BROWN • LIGHT CINNAMON • PAYNE'S GREY • SAPPHIRE • SNOW WHITE • *DecoArt Hot Shots:* FIERY RED

*Royal & Langnickel: Royal Aqualon Wisp* ¹/₄", ³/₈" FILBERT, SERIES R2935 • *Royal Pure Red Sable* 16 SHORT ROUND, SERIES L5005 • *Royal Fusion* 4, 6, 8 SHADER, SERIES 3150 • ²⁰/₀ LINER, SERIES 3585

DECOART AMERICANA MULTI-PURPOSE SEALER, SNOW-TEX, AMERICANA MATTE ACRYLIC SEALER/FINISHER • ROYAL & LANGNICKLE ACRYLIC/OIL DISPOSABLE PALETTE PAPER • BROWN PAPER BAG • WHITE TRANSFER PAPER • STYLUS • TRACING PAPER • ALEENE'S TACKY GLUE • MINI JINGLE BELL • NARROW RED RIBBON • 6" LIGHT GREEN CROCHET COTTON OR STRING • CLEAR FINE GLITTER

# PREPARATION

Seal the ornament with multi-purpose sealer. Base paint the front and back of the ornament with Admiral Blue and a shader. Let dry.

Sand the surface with brown paper bag and apply a second coat of paint. While the paint is still wet, pick up Sapphire in the shader and highlight each point of the snowflake. Blend the two colors together with a light patting motion. Let dry.

Dry brush Baby Blue highlights on the points with a short round brush. With a liner and Baby Blue, carefully paint a thin line around the border of the snowflake. Let dry.

Transfer only the main details of the design with white transfer paper and stylus.

# STEP 1

Base paint the bear's head and ears using an appropriate size filbert wisp brush and Honey Brown. Work in a circle, pulling from the center out to create wispy edge fur. Fill in the entire head and ears.

Without letting the paint dry, and without cleaning the brush, pick up Golden Straw in the brush and highlight the fur. Once again, pull the brush from the center out to the edges. Use lighter pressure on the brush so that the Golden Straw will highlight, rather than cover, the Honey Brown.

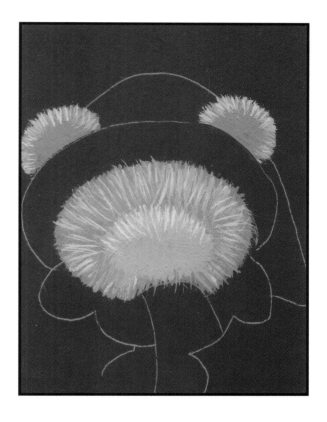

Pick up more Golden Straw, and base paint the muzzle. Use the same technique, pulling from the center to the edges of the oval muzzle shape.

Highlight the top of muzzle, around the face, and tops of ears with French Vanilla and a very light touch.

# STEP 3

Undercoat the top of the hat with Sapphire and a no. 6 shader, then shade with Payne's Grey and highlight with Baby Blue. When dry, dry brush the highlight with a round sable brush and just a bit of Snow White. Outline the top edge of the hat with a thin line of Baby Blue.

Undercoat the hatband with Country Red and a no. 6 shader. Shade with Black Plum and highlight with Fiery Red.

With a liner, add thin vertical lines of Sapphire highlighted with Snow White in the center. Add wider lines of Hauser Medium Green with a no. 4 shader. Highlight the center of the lines with Hauser Medium Green + Snow White. With a liner, over paint thin lines of Snow White on each Hauser Medium Green stripe and add horizontal lines across the hatband.

Lightly dry brush the center area of the hatband and the crown of the hat with a round sable brush and Snow White.

# STEP 2

Shade the fur with a filbert wisp brush of appropriate size and Light Cinnamon. With short strokes, pat the paint into the ears, around the muzzle, and where the forehead meets the hat band. Let dry.

Intensify the shading. Float Light Cinnamon with a no. 6 shader around the muzzle, on top of the lower part of the muzzle, and under the hatband. Shade the top inside of the ears with Bittersweet Chocolate and a no. 4 shader.

Add Bittersweet Chocolate eyes, nose, and mouth, and Light Cinnamon freckles with a liner. With a no. 4 shader, place a Honey Brown c-stroke reflection in the lower left of each eye. With a liner, add a Snow White highlight in the upper right of each eye and on the nose. Paint the lower lip French Vanilla.

Shade under the nose, lips, and each side of the lower lip where it meets the mouth with Light Cinnamon and no. 6 shader.

Dry brush the cheeks with Country Red and a short sable round. Pick up a small amount of paint in the brush. Scrub most of the paint off on a paper towel, then gently scrub remaining color onto the cheeks.

# Step 4

Undercoat the bear's scarf in Hauser Medium Green with a no. 6 shader, and then highlight with Hauser Medium Green + French Vanilla. Shade the scarf with Hauser Dark Green and a no. 6 shader. Add French Vanilla stripes with a liner. Lightly dry brush Snow White on the scarf with a short sable round. Float shading behind bear with a no. 8 shader and Payne's Grey.

With a liner and French Vanilla, soften the shading on the bear's face and ears with a few more highlighted hairs.

# Finishing

Apply sealer/finisher the ornament. Tie a tiny string bow onto the jingle bell, and then glue to end of the hat. Pat Snow-Tex on the top edges of snowflake with a shader. While still wet, sprinkle with glitter. Add a narrow red ribbon to hang the ornament.

# Christmas Holly

Jo Avis Moore

# MATERIALS

*Delta Ceramcoat Acrylics:* LIGHT IVORY • *Archival Oil Colors:* BURNT UMBER • CADMIUM ORANGE • CADMIUM RED LIGHT • CADMIUM YELLOW LIGHT • FRENCH ULTRAMARINE BLUE • MARS BLACK • PERMANENT ALIZARINE • PURPLE • RAW SIENNA DARK • TITANIUM WHITE • *Archival:* CLASSIC MEDIUM

*Royal & Langnickel:* Kolinsky Elite 2, 4, 6, 12 CHISEL SHADER, SERIES: R6150-S • 1, 2 SCRIPT LINER, SERIES R6585

TURPENOID ODORLESS THINNER • LIBERTY MATTE FINISH SPRAY • 400 GRIT SANDPAPER • TRACING PAPER • GRAY TRANSFER PAPER • STYLUS • PALETTE KNIFE • SOFT CLOTH • GOLD CORD • KRYLON 18 KT. GOLD LEAFING PEN

# PREPARATION

Sand the porcelain ornament lightly with 400 grit sandpaper. Remove sanding dust. Seal the entire ornament with several light coats of matte finish spray. Dry thoroughly.

Base paint the entire ornament with two coats of Light Ivory acrylic paint and a no. 12 chisel shader. Let dry between coats.

When dry, sand the base painted surface lightly with 400 grit sandpaper. Spray very lightly with matte finish spray and dry thoroughly before applying the pattern. This is very important.

Trace and transfer the design with gray transfer paper and a stylus. Since this is a very small ornament, apply the pattern carefully. Keep transfer lines as pale as possible.

# TECHNIQUE

Undercoat the holly sprig with appropriate size chisel shaders. Add shading, and then highlights. Enhance the highlights and add tints. Tuck shading where the leaves overlap and behind the berries. Look for good contrast of lights and darks in your painting in order to create form and interest. Refine as much as needed.

Detail the painting with appropriate size script liners. Thin the paint with odorless thinner for fine lines.

# STEP 1

Undercoat the leaves with a medium value green mix of Cadmium Yellow Light + Mars Black (3:1) + a touch Titanium White + a touch French Ultramarine Blue. Use a no. 6 chisel shader for the large leaves and a no. 4 chisel shader for the small leaves.

Undercoat the berries with Cadmium Red Light + Permanent Alizarine (1:1), and the branch with Raw Sienna Dark + Mars Black (1:1).

# STEP 3

Reinforce the dark side of the leaves with more Mars Black.

Build highlights on the opposite side of each leaf with Titanium White. Stroke veins on the leaves with a no. 1 script liner and thinned Titanium White.

Highlight the branch with Titanium White, and the berries with Cadmium Orange + Titanium White.

# STEP 2

Shade the leaves along the central vein with medium value green mix + Mars Black and a chisel shader.

Highlight the opposite side of each leaf with medium value green mix + Titanium White.

Shade the holly berries with Purple.

# STEP 4

If needed, enhance the light and dark values of the leaves. Study the painting, looking for good darks and lights. Try to have a glint of pure color somewhere in an object. Check triangle areas, shading more if necessary to achieve another value. The more values present in an object, the more realistic it becomes.

Place tints of warm and cool color in the leaves. Use brush mixed Cadmium Orange + Cadmium Red Light for warm accents, and Titanium White + French Ultramarine Blue for cooler accents.

Add a small Mars Black dot to each berry with a script liner.

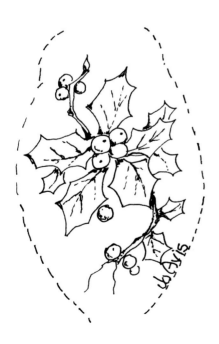

# FINISHING

Finish the ends of the ornament with the red berry and green leaf color mixes. Let the painting dry.

Add gold embellishments with a gold leafing pen.

Seal the painting with several light coats of matte finish spray. Use gold cord to hang.

*Deck the halls
with boughs of holly ...*

# Angel Dust

Cynthia Erekson

# MATERIALS

*DecoArt Americana Acrylics:* BLACK PLUM • BLEACHED SAND • BLUE/GREY MIST • CAMEL • CHARCOAL GREY • DEEP BURGUNDY • DOVE GREY • DUSTY ROSE • HONEY BROWN • LAMP BLACK • MARIGOLD • SHADING FLESH • UNIFORM BLUE • WARM WHITE • *DecoArt Dazzling Metallics:* SHIMMERING SILVER • SPLENDID GOLD • *Jo Sonja's:* CLEAR GLAZE MEDIUM • FLOW MEDIUM • OPAL DUST

*Silver Brush, Ltd:* Ultra Mini 8, 10, 14 DESIGNER ROUND, SERIES 2431S • ²⁰⁄₀ SCRIPT LINER, SERIES 2407S • *Scharff:* WHITE BRISTLE MOON 2, 4, 6 FILBERT, SERIES 222 • OLD SCRUFFY FLAT BRUSH • ¹/₂" SOFT STENCIL BRUSH • TWO 1" SPONGE BRUSHES

DECOART AMERICANA MATTE ACRYLIC SEALER/FINISHER • FINE SANDPAPER • TRACING PAPER • WHITE AND GRAY TRANSFER PAPER • STYLUS • KNEADED ERASER • WAXED PALETTE PAD • PALETTE KNIFE • EMPTY CARDBOARD PAPER TOWEL ROLL • 6" SQUARE FIBERGLASS SCREENING • INDEX CARD • ALEENE'S THICK DESIGNER TACKY GLUE • ¹/₈" MASONITE SWAG CURTAIN CUT-OUT • SMALL ¹/₂" LASER CUT WOODEN SNOWFLAKE • 8" GOLD CORD

# PREPARATION

Lightly sand all surfaces. Base paint the front and cut edges of the ornament square and the curtain with a sponge brush and Lamp Black. Apply one coat of Blue/Grey Mist over the Lamp Black on the front of the square. Base paint the back of the square with Deep Burgundy.

With sponge brush, press and lift Deep Burgundy onto the front side of the window frame to create texture. Let dry and repeat. Paint all cut edges of the frame Lamp Black.

# TECHNIQUE

Apply undercoats with an appropriate size designer round. To prevent shapes from growing, first outline all buildings and roofs with the tip of the brush, then carefully fill in with horizontal strokes.

Use an appropriate size moon brush to dry brush shading and highlighting. Load the brush, then remove some paint by stroking the brush on a paper towel. Apply color by scrubbing side to side with the chisel edge. Pull the color out from the shaded or highlighted area to soften hard edges. Paint details and linework with a script liner.

# STEP 1

Sand the background with the grain of wood, exposing bits of black. Trace and transfer the design. Undercoat the ground with streaky Dove Grey. Let background show through for shadows. Erase transfer lines.

Load a stencil brush with Shimmering Silver. Wipe off most of the paint on a paper towel. Lightly scrub the brush side to side over the sky and snow. Highlight along the hills and randomly about the ground with Splendid Gold.

Undercoat the moon Splendid Gold, the bowl Marigold, the dress Deep Burgundy, and the wing Dove Grey. Shade the wing with Charcoal Grey and the bowl with Honey Brown.

Fill the inside of the bowl with Honey Brown. Line bowl rim with Camel. Highlight bowl on upper right with Camel.

# STEP 3

Outline roofs with Lamp Black. Fill in horizontally, leaving a bit of basecoat color showing in roof centers. Dry brush these area with Splendid Gold.

Shade Charcoal Grey building with Lamp Black and others with Charcoal Grey. Place the edge of an index card along the edge to be shaded. Lightly scrub along edge of card with a no. 2 moon brush. Press brush onto card and lightly pull color across shaded side of building. With vertical liner strokes, add Lamp Black windows, a Deep Burgundy door on the right building, and other doors of Lamp Black. Keep windows and doors small for a primitive look. Color chimneys Deep Burgundy plus Black Plum (1:1) with a script liner.

Mound snow under houses and throughout ground by touching down with the chisel edge of the no. 6 moon brush loaded with Bleached Sand.

Create Charcoal Grey trees with the tip of no. 8 designer round. Add a squiggly line on right sides of trunks and branches with Bleached Sand. Mound snow under trees. Tap foliage sparsely onto trees with Bleached Sand and an old scruffy flat brush. Add Warm White to the dirty brush and tap onto foliage to brighten some areas.

Gently spatter the scene with Warm White snowflakes. Load the stencil brush with thinned paint and flick the bristles using a palette knife.

# STEP 2

Shade moon Deep Burgundy. Add a Deep Burgundy line along right side of moon. Stripe the bowl with Uniform Blue and Bleached Sand. Add feet and hands with Shading Flesh. Dab on a wash of Dusty Rose. Undercoat head Dusty Rose. Wash top of head and cheek with Shading Flesh.

Place Bleached Sand strokes on the wing with a liner. Shade the dress Black Plum. Highlight the dress with Deep Burgundy plus a touch of Bleached Sand on the dirty brush. Line under the sleeve, ends of sleeves along pleats, and hem of dress with Black Plum. Paint collar Black Plum. Line dress stripes Honey Brown.

Line Halo with Bleached Sand. Dab on Splendid Gold here and there with the tip of the liner. Place a Splendid Gold dot under the chin with a stylus.

With appropriate colors, undercoat the buildings and roofs. Shade beneath the buildings with Blue/Grey Mist.

# STEP 4

Place screening straight on the swag. Load a stencil brush with Honey Brown. Remove some paint on a paper towel. Pounce dry color through the screen. Repeat several times to build up color. Add Marigold to the dirty brush and remove some paint. Pounce in highlight areas. Remove screen.

Shade the curtain with dry brushed Lamp Black. Highlight the folds with dry brushed Marigold. Create small Lamp Black inner folds on the bottom of curtain. Add a Lamp Black tieback with a Deep Burgundy stripe. Dry brush inner cut edges of the curtain with Honey Brown and a moon brush.

Paint the top side of the snowflake cut-out with Camel and spatter with Warm White.

# FINISHING

Create a faux woodgrain window frame with Lamp Black, Clear Glaze Medium and flow medium (1:8:2). Press the mix onto the frame with a sponge brush. Roll a cardboard tube diagonally across the frame. Roll again in another direction. Lightly tap with a moon brush to soften pattern. When dry, trim the frame with Lamp Black.

Brush on Opal Dust streaming from the angel's bowl. Spray ornament pieces with two coats of matte sealer/finisher. Assemble ornament with thin layers of glue. Insert gold cord between window square and frame.

2009 Cynthia Erekson

*Spread some angel dust today ...*
*Send your troubles on their way.*

97

# Peep Peep

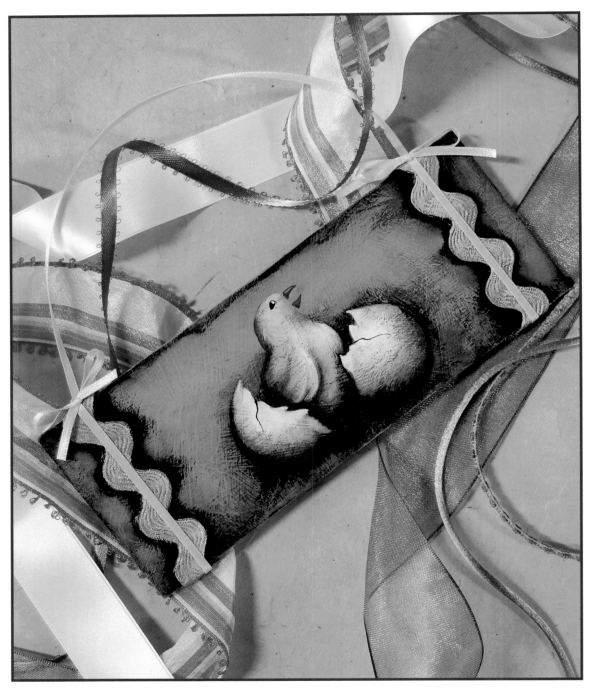

Andy Jones

# MATERIALS

*Plaid FolkArt Artists' Pigments:* BURNT SIENNA • BURNT UMBER • DIOXAZINE PURPLE • HAUSER GREEN LIGHT • PURE BLACK • TITANIUM WHITE • YELLOW LIGHT • YELLOW OCHRE

*Silver Brush, Ltd.: Golden Natural* 4, 8 SHADER, SERIES 2002S • 2 SCRIPT LINER, SERIES 2007S • ¾" WASH, SERIES 2008S • *Ruby Satin* 8 FILBERT, SERIES 2503S • *PCM Studios* 1" GLAZE VARNISH, SERIES 1414S

PLAID FOLKART CLEARCOTE MATTE ACRYLIC SEALER • COTMAN SEPIA WATERCOLOR • OLD WAX COATED PALETTE • PALETTE KNIFE • PAPER TOWELS • WOOD FILLER • FINE GRIT SANDPAPER • TRACING PAPER • FINE TIP MARKER • BALLPOINT PEN • WHITE TRANSFER PAPER • OLD FACE CLOTH • DISHWASHING LIQUID • WHITE CRAFT GLUE • LAVENDER RICKRACK TRIM • YELLOW RIBBON

# PREPARATION

Fill in small holes on the wooden ornament with wood filler. Dry, and sand lightly.

Base paint the entire ornament with a light green mix of Hauser Green Light + Yellow Light (2:1) and a glaze varnish brush loaded with an ample amount of paint. Apply the paint in a slip-slap motion. Leave some visible brush marks. Let dry. Apply a second coat if needed.

Glue rickrack trim onto the ornament with white glue. Let dry.

Trace the design with a fine tip marker. Transfer the design with white transfer paper and a ballpoint pen.

# TECHNIQUE

Undercoat and shade the design elements. Develop highlights with a dry brush technique. Antique the design to add depth and emphasize the folk art look, then freshen the highlights and add details.

Select brushes of appropriate size and style for each step. Use the largest brush that can be easily manipulated in each area.

# STEP 1

Use a completely dry shader to opaquely undercoat the design elements. Undercoat the eggshells with a light gray mix of Titanium White + Burnt Umber + Pure Black (4:1:1). Undercoat the chick with Yellow Ochre + Yellow Light (1:1) and the beak with Burnt Sienna. Let dry completely.

Shade the chick with Burnt Sienna and the eggshells with Pure Black + Burnt Umber (2:1). Heavily side load the shader with opaque color on one edge. Avoid floating several layers of color to achieve the desired darkness. Study the worksheet to see the amount of shading needed prior to antiquing.

remain slightly visible. If the watercolor creeps, add a drop or two of dishwashing liquid. The soap will cause the paint to flow out smoothly. Avoid the rickrack trim.

Once the watercolor is dry, begin to remove it. Dampen an old face cloth and wring it out well. The cloth should be barely damp, not wet. Fold the cloth into a soft pad and begin to wipe away the antiquing. The damp cloth will remove the watercolor. Change the cloth often in order not to redeposit color where it is not wanted. Remove enough color from the piece to reveal the design, but remain dark at the edges.

Wrap a fresh part of the cloth around your index finger. Remove the antiquing from the highlighted area of the design and the background. Frequently change to a clean portion of the rag. Leave the antiquing darker in the shadow areas of the design.

When satisfied with the antiquing, allow it to rest for a few minutes. If too much color was removed, apply more Sepia. If not pleased with the results, wet the cloth, wash off all of the antiquing, and try again.

Since the antiquing is done with watercolor and would wash off if a water-based varnish were applied, seal the painting with several light coats of matte acrylic spray sealer.

# STEP 2

Highlight the chick and eggshells with a dry filbert and a scant amount of color. Build highlights gradually. Begin each highlight in the brightest area. Observe that as highlights get lighter, they also get smaller.

Dry brush the eggshells first with the undercoat mix, then add Titanium White highlights. Dry brush the chick with the undercoat mix, then with undercoat mix + Yellow Light. Continue building highlights with Yellow Light, then Yellow Light + Titanium White. Add more Titanium White as needed to brighten highlights.

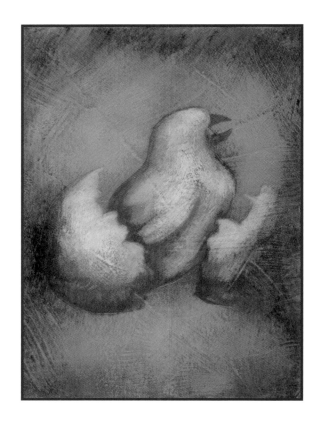

# STEP 3

Antique the ornament with the following technique. The watercolor-based process is a bit unusual, but adds a nice folk art quality to the ornament.

Apply a thin, even coat of Sepia watercolor to the ornament, one section at a time, with a wash brush. The watercolor should be the consistency of thin syrup. The painted design should

# STEP 4

Lightly freshen highlights and add details to the antiqued painting. Resist repainting the image.

Complete the eggshells with a light gray mix of Titanium White + a touch Pure Black + a touch Burnt Umber. Further highlight the shells with more Titanium White. Add fine cracks to the shells with Burnt Umber + Pure Black and a script liner.

Develop the chick highlights with Yellow Light, then add Titanium White. Highlight the beak with Burnt Sienna + Titanium White. Add the Burnt Umber + Pure Black eye. Highlight with a dot of Titanium White.

Brush accents on the rickrack trim with a filbert and various mixes of Titanium White + Dioxazine Purple.

# FINISHING

Apply several coats of matte acrylic spray sealer. Attach yellow ribbons with white craft glue.

# Moonlit Evening

Jamie Mills-Price

# MATERIALS

*DecoArt Americana Acrylics:* BLEACHED SAND • BURNT ORANGE • BURNT UMBER • JADE GREEN • LAMP BLACK • NEUTRAL GREY • PAYNE'S GREY • PLANTATION PINE • ROYAL PURPLE • UNIFORM BLUE • WARM WHITE • YELLOW OCHRE

*Jo Sonja's: Sure Touch* 6 OVAL DRY BRUSH, SERIES 2010 • 6, 10 FLAT, SERIES 1370 • 6, 8 FILBERT, SERIES 1385 • 3 ROUND, SERIES 1350 • *Loew-Cornell: La Corneille Golden Taklon* ¹⁸/₀ LINER, SERIES 7350 • *Maxine's* ¹/₂" MOP, SERIES 270

DECOART SNOW-TEX, STAR LITE VARNISH, DURACLEAR MATTE VARNISH • TRACING PAPER • WHITE AND GRAY TRANSFER PAPER • STYLUS • WAX COATED PALETTE • ASSORTED RIBBONS

# PREPARATION

Base paint the front and back round sections of the ornament with a no. 8 filbert and Uniform Blue tipped in Warm White. Move the brush back and forth in a diagonal, slip-slap fashion.

Base paint the bow and sides of the ornament with a no. 8 filbert and Bleached Sand. Let dry.

Trace the pattern on tracing paper. Transfer the pattern for the moon, mountains, snowy hills, and snowman with white transfer paper and a stylus. Omit details at this time.

# TECHNIQUE

Refer to the inked dots on the pattern for specific shading placement if it is not noted in the instructions.

Float highlights and shading with a flat brush. After you have placed the float, use a dry ¹/₂" mop to soften the strokes. Move the brush in an up-and-down motion, working from the water area in toward the paint.

# STEP 1

Undercoat the snowman with a no. 6 filbert and Bleached Sand. With the same brush, undercoat the mountains with Royal Purple tipped in Warm White.

Undercoat the moon with a no. 3 round and Bleached Sand, tipped in Yellow Ochre. The moon does not have to have opaque coverage.

# STEP 3

Add snowman details with a liner. Paint the features and button Lamp Black and the nose Burnt Orange. Highlight the nose with Warm White. Stroke in the tied bow with Royal Purple tipped in Warm White. Paint the stick arms Burnt Umber tipped in Bleached Sand.

Tap in the evergreen wreath with a liner loaded with Plantation Pine and tipped in Warm White.

Paint the tree trunks with Burnt Umber and a liner. While wet tip the brush in Warm White and highlight.

# STEP 2

Float shading on the snowman using a no. 10 flat sideloaded with Neutral Grey. With the same brush, side-load and float a tint of Royal Purple on the left side of the snowman's belly and right shoulder.

Sideload the brush with Warm White and float highlights on the snowman, moon, mountaintops, and the snowy ground.

Sideload the brush with Yellow Ochre. Float a glow around the moon. Let dry.

Transfer the pattern for the trees with white transfer paper, and the pattern for the snowman's features, arms, bow, buttons, arms, and wreath with gray transfer paper.

# STEP 4

Doubleload a no. 6 filbert with Jade Green + Plantation Pine. Blend on the palette. Tip the Jade Green side in Warm White and blend again. Tap tree branches on the tree trunks. Work from bottom to top, using a horizontal movement. Wash the brush and sideload with Warm White. Tap over the trees to add further highlights.

Sideload a no. 10 flat with a bit of Snow-Tex and accent snowy hills, under the snowman, and mountaintops.

Sideload a no. 10 flat with Payne's Grey and float around the perimeter of the round section. Dry brush the recessed border with Warm White and a no. 6 oval dry brush. Add Warm White dots with a stylus.

Stripe the ornament sides and top bow with a no. 6 flat and thinned Royal Purple. Line between the stripes with a liner and Uniform Blue. With a no. 10 flat, float Royal Purple shading and Warm White highlights.

# FINISHING

Personalize the back of the ornament as desired.

Apply matte varnish to the ornament with a no. 10 flat, following the manufacturer's instructions.

Optional Finish: Load a no. 6 filbert with Star Lite Varnish. Tap over the snow.

Embellish the ornament with assorted ribbons.

# Korny Friend

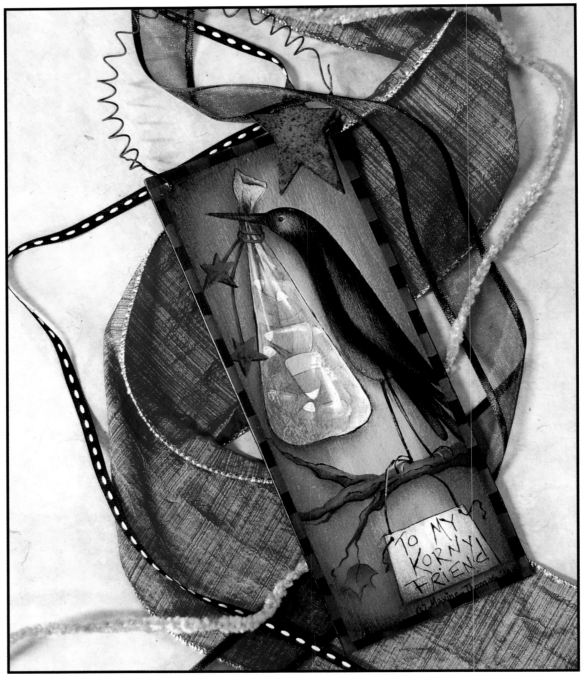

Maxine Thomas

# MATERIALS

*DecoArt American Acrylics:* BURNT ORANGE • BURNT SIENNA • DARK CHOCOLATE • HONEY BROWN • KHAKI TAN • LAMP BLACK • LIGHT BUTTERMILK • MARIGOLD • RUSSET • SLATE GREY • SOFT BLACK • *Weber Professional Permalba Oil Colors:* BURNT UMBER

*Loew-Cornell: La Corneille Golden Taklon* 4 FILBERT, SERIES 7500 • 12 FLAT SHADER, SERIES 7300 • <sup>10</sup>/o LINER, SERIES 7350 • *Maxine's* <sup>3</sup>/8" MOP, SERIES 270

DECOART AMERICANA MULTI-PURPOSE SEALER, AMERICANA MATTE ACRYLIC SEALER/FINISHER • ALEENE'S TACKY GLUE • TRACING PAPER • WHITE TRANSFER PAPER • STYLUS • SANDPAPER • SOFT CLOTH • WAX COATED PALETTE • ODORLESS THINNER • 1<sup>3</sup>/4" RUSTY STAR • RUSTY WIRE

# PREPARATION

Lightly sand the wooden ornament. Remove dust with a damp cloth. Seal the wood with multi-purpose sealer. Let dry.

Base paint the back and front of the surface with Khaki Tan. Let dry thoroughly.

Trace the design and transfer the main pattern lines with white transfer paper and a stylus.

# TECHNIQUE

Undercoat the basic elements of the design with a smooth opaque coat of color. When dry, shade and highlight the design with floats of color. Gently tap floated color with a mop to soften any harsh lines of color at the outer edges.

Select brushes of appropriate size and style for each step described in the instructions.

# STEP 1

Undercoat the crow's body with Lamp Black. Leave the white transfer line of the wing exposed.

Undercoat the centers of the candy corn with Burnt Orange, tips with Light Buttermilk , and bottoms with Marigold. Leave the transfer lines between the candy corn shapes visible. Undercoat the spaces around the candies with Russet.

Streakily undercoat the branch with Dark Chocolate. Undercoat the sign with Light Buttermilk, the leaf with Burnt Orange, and the stars with Burnt Sienna.

## STEP 3

Stroke Light Buttermilk highlights on the candy corns. Let dry Create the bag over the corn area and above the beak with a wash of Light Buttermilk. Let dry.

Dry brush Slate Grey highlights on the crow's beak, head stomach, wing, and tail feathers.

Highlight the center of the branch with Honey Brown and th tip of leaf with Marigold. Highlight the stars and the upper righ and front of the sign wire with Burnt Orange.

## STEP 2

Shade between the candy corn pieces and along the top of the leaf with Russet. Shade along the bottoms of the branches and dab texture on the stars with Soft Black. Let dry.

*Candy corn was invented in the 1880's. Celebrate National Candy Corn Day on October 30 !*

# FINISHING

Shade the background with Dark Chocolate. Accent where needed with Lamp Black lines. Freehand a checked border of Lamp Black and Burnt Orange. Let dry.

Use your favorite method to antique the surface with Burnt Umber oil paint. Spray with several coats of sealer/finisher. Glue the rusty star to the corner and attach the wire.

# STEP 4

With Soft Black, shade the bag opening at the top, and in the feathers above and below the crow's beak. Highlight the front of the opening, along the gathers, and at the bottom right of the bag with Light Buttermilk.

Dot the crow's eye with Marigold and add a smaller dot of Lamp Black for the pupil. With a liner and Lamp Black, paint the legs and feet. Highlight the center of the legs and tops of the toes with Slate Grey.

With a liner and Lamp Black thinned with water, create grain lines in the branch, add a vein to the leaf, and paint the wire, holes, and words on the sign. Place skipped highlights along the wire with Slate Grey.

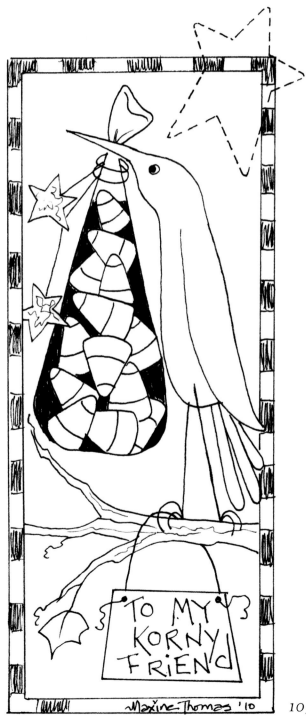

# Freedom Rings

Toni McGuire

# MATERIALS

*DecoArt Americana Acrylics:* BURNT UMBER • ICE BLUE • LIGHT BUTTERMILK • PAYNE'S GREY • RAW SIENNA • SANTA RED • SOFT BLACK • TRUE BLUE •
*DecoArt Dazzling Metallics:* CHAMPAGNE GOLD • VENETIAN GOLD

*JoSonja's: Sure Touch* 4, 6, 10 FLAT, SERIES 1370 • *Silver Brush, Ltd.: Ultra Mini* 2 DESIGNER ROUND, SERIES 2431S • OLD SCRUFFY BRUSH • SMALL MOP

DECOART AMERICANA MATTE ACRYLIC SEALER/FINISHER • RUST-OLEUM CLEAN METAL PRIMER SPRAY • TRACING PAPER • WHITE TRANSFER PAPER • STYLUS • WAX COATED PALETTE • PATRIOTIC RIBBON • JEWELRY CHARMS

# PREPARATION

Prepare the tin ornament with primer spray following the manufacturer's instructions.

When it is thoroughly dry, opaquely base paint the entire surface with three to four coats of Payne's Grey. Allow adequate drying time between coats.

Transfer the design using white transfer paper and a stylus.

# TECHNIQUE

Undercoat design elements with a flat brush of appropriate size and smooth opaque color. When dry, float highlights and shadows to add dimension to the shapes.

Rinse a flat brush in clean water, pat dry on a paper towel, then side load the brush with color. Blend the color well on a wax coated palette before moving on to the surface.

Dampen the underlying surface with clean water before applying the float of color to soften the effect if you are heavy handed with the application.

Gently tap floated color with a mop to soften any harsh lines of color at the outer edges. Gradually build light floats of color, allowing ample drying time between layers.

# STEP 1

Undercoat the bell and clapper with Venetian Gold and the wooden yoke with Burnt Umber. Undercoat the metal bolts on the yoke with Venetian Gold and the straps with Raw Sienna.

When dry, transfer the bands and crack on the bell with the white transfer paper. Paint these lines, as well as the lines on the bolts, with a designer round and Payne's Grey thinned with water. Create the wood grain with thinned Burnt Umber + Soft Black (1:1) and a designer round.

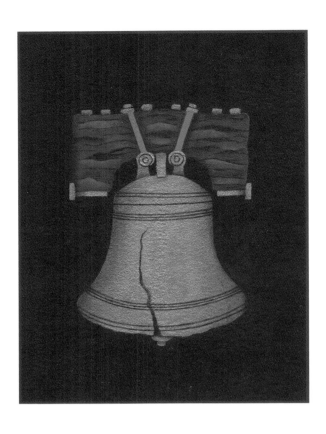

# Step 3

Create the illusion of reflected light with a light float of Ice Blue along the right edge of the bell. Float a small accent highlight of Venetian Gold with a no. 4 flat between the set of bands along the lower left edge of the bell. Lightly float Raw Sienna along the right side of the yoke with a no. 6 flat.

Shade the straps on the yoke at the top and bottom with Burnt Umber and a no. 4 flat. Highlight the center of each strap with a liner and Light Buttermilk.

Transfer the lettering with the white transfer paper, and then line with Venetian Gold.

# Step 2

Highlight the center of the bell with "back to back" floats of Champagne Gold using a no. 6 flat or, if you prefer, dry brush the highlight with an old scruffy brush.

Float shading along the edges of the bell with a no. 10 flat. Several light floats are preferable to one heavy float in order to achieve a more realistic look. Shade the bolts and clapper with side loaded floats of Payne's Grey and a no. 4 flat.

Highlight the yoke with Raw Sienna floats. In the same manner, shade the yoke with Burnt Umber + Soft Black (1:1).

## FINISHING

When painting is complete, spray with several light coats of sealer/finisher. Embellish with ribbon and jewelry accents.

## STEP 4

Create ¼" Santa Red borders on both sides of the ornament. Several coats will be needed for the color to become opaque. Let dry thoroughly.

Transfer the stars with white transfer paper and paint with Light Buttermilk. Add True Blue lines between the stars. Place dots on top of these lines with a stylus and Venetian Gold. Do not thin paint for stylus dots. Line along the inside edge of the red border with True Blue.

Undercoat the star design on the back of the ornament with Venetian Gold. When dry, transfer the interior lines and outline them with Payne's Grey. Create dimensional shading on the star with Payne's Grey floats and a no. 6 flat.

Transfer the circle around the large star and line with Santa Red. With a no. 10 flat, float the same color around the inside of the circle. Dot the circle and create linework designs in the corners with Venetian Gold. Accent with True Blue dots.

Toni McGuire
2009

113

# Christmas Puppy

Karen Hubbard

# MATERIALS

*DecoArt Americana Acrylics*: BITTERSWEET CHOCOLATE • BLUE CHIFFON • GOLDEN STRAW • HONEY BROWN • MILK CHOCOLATE • NAVY BLUE • SNOW WHITE • TAFFY CREAM

*ReKab*: *Red Sable* 4 ROUND, SERIES 013 • *Scharff*: *Red Sable* 2 SCROLLER, SERIES 470 • *Royal & Langnickel*: *Majestic* 6, 10 SHADER, SERIES 4150 • *Robert Simmons*: *Expression* 3/4" FLAT WASH/GLAZE, SERIES E55

DECOART AMERICANA MATTE ACRYLIC SEALER/FINISHER • 600 GRIT LIGHT COLORED SANDPAPER • TRACING PAPER • GRAY TRANSFER PAPER • STYLUS • FINE-POINT BLACK MARKER • SCOTCH MAGIC TAPE • MASTERSON STA-WET PALETTE • CLEAR FINE SPRINKLE GLITTER • SOFT CLOTH

# PREPARATION

Lightly sand the porcelain ornament with fine grit sandpaper. Remove the sanding dust. Base paint with a flat wash/glaze brush and one thin coat of Blue Chiffon. When dry, apply a second coat. Sand again lightly.

Carefully trace the pattern onto tracing paper with a fine-point marker. Position the pattern on the ornament and tape securely. Transfer only the outline of the pup and bow with a stylus and gray transfer paper. Leave pattern attached for transferring details later.

# TECHNIQUE

Use a no. 4 round sable brush to create the look of fur. Wet the brush, then blot on a paper towel, leaving the brush slightly damp. Flatten the bristles as you fill the brush, making sure the bristles are coated with paint up into the center of the brush. Use a wet palette so that some water will gradually mix with the paint and thin it slightly.

Apply soft pressure at the heel of the loaded brush to spread the bristles. The brush should look flat and fanned out, resembling a small fan brush. Hold the brush at the top of the ferrule at a 45-degree angle to the surface and pull the brush stroke with a small sweeping motion. Brush strokes should look like a cluster of tiny lines.

Float all shading with a side loaded shader brush.

# STEP 1

Undercoat the pup with Honey Brown and a round sable brush. If needed, repeat to cover. Undercoat the bow with a mix of Navy Blue + Blue Chiffon (1:1).

When dry, transfer the pattern details using a stylus and gray transfer paper.

Basecoat the nose and iris with Milk Chocolate, and the pupil and nostrils with Bittersweet Chocolate. Shade the bow with Navy Blue and a no. 6 shader.

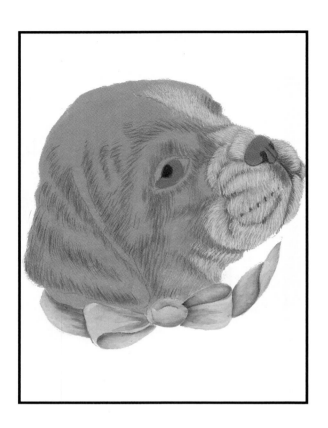

# STEP 3

Float shading on brown fur areas with a no. 10 shader and Mil[k] Chocolate. Shade the top of the eye and into the front corner[s] around the nose, and the mouth area with a no. 6 shader an[d] Bittersweet Chocolate.

Highlight all the remaining open brown areas with Golden Stra[w] fur strokes.

Float light bow edges with a no. 10 shader and Blue Chiffon.

# STEP 2

With a round sable brush, paint Bittersweet Chocolate fur strokes on fur pattern lines as described in the Technique section.

Fill white fur areas with Taffy Cream fur strokes.

Outline the nose, detail the mouth, and add whisker dots with Bittersweet Chocolate and a no. 2 scroller.

# STEP 4

Darken brown fur shading with Bittersweet Chocolate. Highlight white fur with Snow White fur strokes. Highlight brown fur with Taffy Cream fur strokes.

Line the edge of the lower eyelid with thin Bittersweet Chocolate and a scroller. Add a touch of Golden Straw in the center of the lower part of the iris. With a no. 6 shader, float a tiny bit of Snow White at the front corner of the eye. Add a Snow White sparkle in the eye and a tiny line at the lower left lid with a scroller.

With a stylus, add graduated dots of Snow White along the edges of the bow. Create tiny white snowflakes on the bow and a few blue snowflakes around the pup with a scroller.

Float very transparent Navy Blue next to the muzzle and under the blue bow.

# FINISHING

Lightly spray the ornament with matte sealer/finisher. While still wet, sprinkle with a little clear glitter. Let dry.

Spray with another two coats of sealer/finisher.

Karen Hubbard

# Overstuffed

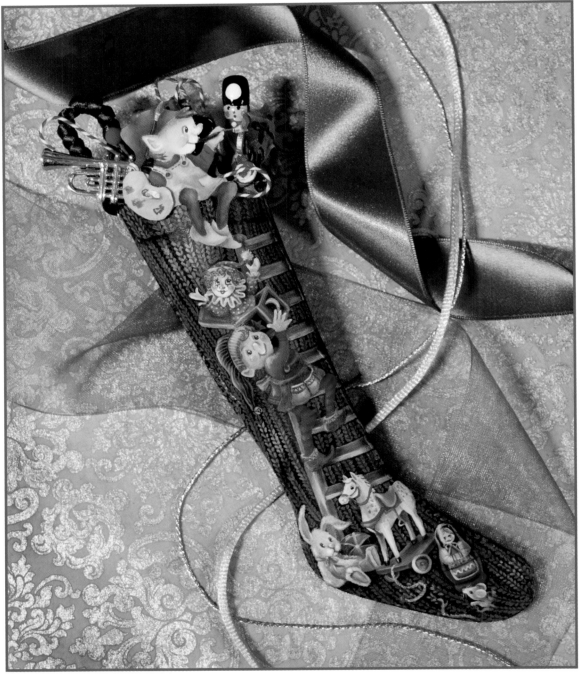

Tina Sue Norris

# MATERIALS

*DecoArt Americana Acrylics:* DEEP TEAL • DOVE GREY • GOLDEN STRAW • HI-LITE FLESH • KHAKI TAN • MISSISSIPPI MUD • NEUTRAL GREY • SABLE BROWN • TOMATO RED • VIOLET HAZE • SNOW WHITE • *Winsor & Newton Griffin Alkyd Oil Colours:* BURNT SIENNA • BURNT UMBER • CADMIUM RED MEDIUM • CADMIUM YELLOW MEDIUM • DIOXAZINE PURPLE • FLESH TINT • IVORY BLACK • PRUSSIAN BLUE • RAW UMBER • TERRA VERTE • TITANIUM WHITE

*Tina Designs:* 2, 4 CAT'S TONGUE FILBERT • *Loew-Cornell: La Corneille Golden Taklon* 0 JACKIE SHAW LINER, SERIES JSC • ¹⁰/₀ LINER, SERIES 7350C

FLOOD EASY SURFACE PREP • ALCOHOL • RUST-OLEUM MATTE BLACK SPRAY • WHITE AND GRAY TRANSFER PAPER • STYLUS • WAXED PALETTE • PALETTE KNIFE • TRACING PAPER • FINE POINT PEN • TAPE • SMALL SCISSORS • SOFT CLOTH • ODORLESS THINNER • SPRAY VARNISH • 3" SQUARE MULTIMEDIA BOARD OR HEAVY WATERCOLOR PAPER • BOND 527 CLEAR GLUE • 4" SATIN CORDING • 3" FINE CHAIN • 2 MINI BELLS • 2 CHARMS • ASSORTED CHRISTMAS MINI TOYS • SMALL PIECE STYROFOAM

# PREPARATION

Clean the metal ornament with Easy Surface Prep or alcohol and a soft cloth. Wait 30 minutes, then spray with matte black spray paint. Dry thoroughly. Transfer the ornament pattern with white transfer paper. Transfer the cut-out elf and Santa's list to multimedia board or watercolor paper, with gray transfer paper. Place in warm water for five to ten minutes, then cut out the pieces with small scissors. Fold over the top of the list and hold in place with tape. Allow to dry.

# TECHNIQUE

Alkyds are somewhat translucent. When working on a black surface undercoat, paint the major portion of the pattern using a middle value hue of acrylics. Use alkyds to shade and highlight over the acrylic undercoats.

# STEP 1

Undercoat each of the largest shapes with an appropriate size and style of brush and a light coat of acrylic color as shown in the photo.

Hi-Lite Flesh: elf faces/hands, doll face
Dove Grey: horse, mouse, clown face/hands/collar
Khaki Tan: cut-out elf apron/shoes, bunny
Sable Brown: horse cart/saddle, paintbrush bristles, clown box
Mississippi Mud: ladder, horse cart wheels, palette
Tomato Red: elf shirts/leggings, doll skirt, 2 ball sections, clown box stripe
Deep Teal: elf apron/hats/leggings/shoes, 2 ball sections
Violet Haze: clown suit, doll apron
Golden Straw: clown ruffle, doll arms, hat bells

Burnt Umber: Horse cart/saddle - shade with Burnt Umber highlight with Burnt Umber + Titanium White (2:1).

Cadmium Red Medium: Elf red shirts/leggings - shade with Cadmium Red Medium - darken shading with Cadmium Red Medium + Ivory Black (3:1) - highlight with Cadmium Red Medium + Cadmium Yellow Medium (3:1).

Terra Verte: Elf green hats/apron/leggings/shoes - shade with Terra Verte + Ivory Black (3:1) - highlight with Terra Verte Titanium White (3:1) - blend where colors meet.

Dioxazine Purple: Clown suit/hat and doll apron - shade with Dioxazine Purple + Titanium White (3:1) + a touch Raw Umber.

Allow the alkyds to dry overnight before proceeding.

# $S$TEP 2

Shade and highlight the acrylic undercoats with alkyds as shown in the photo. Use the no. 2 cat's tongue for large areas and the no. $^{10}/_{0}$ liner for features and smallest areas.

Flesh Tint: Elf faces/hands and doll face - shade with Flesh Tint + Burnt Sienna (2:1) - highlight with Flesh Tint + Titanium White - indicate placement of facial features with a liner and Burnt Sienna.

Titanium White: Clown face/hands - shade with Titanium White + Ivory Black (4:1). Horse - shade with same mix + a touch Raw Umber - add Ivory Black to mix and deepen leg shading - highlight with Titanium White. Mouse - shade with Titanium White + Ivory Black (4:1) - highlight with Titanium White.

Raw Umber: Ladder and clown box - shade with Raw Umber, then Raw Umber + Titanium White (2:1) on light edges and rails - highlight lightest edges with Titanium White. Bunny - shade with Raw Umber + Titanium White (2:1) - highlight with Titanium White - add Titanium White + Flesh Tint (3:1) ears/nose/feet. Cut-out elf - shade apron/shoes with Raw Umber.

# STEP 3

Use a liner to paint fine details. Thin the paint with odorless thinner as needed.

Elves: Mouth/nose/ear lines - Burnt Sienna. Hair - Burnt Umber. Eyes - Ivory Black. Paintbrushes - Ivory Black handles, Titanium White + Ivory Black ferrules, Burnt Sienna bristles. Khaki apron - Burnt Umber stitches, Cadmium Red Medium buttons. Palette - red, blue and green paint spots. Red leggings elf - Cadmium Red Medium + Ivory Black (3:1) legging stripes, Cadmium Red Medium apron detail lines, Titanium White hat stripes, Cadmium Yellow Medium bells with Ivory Black shading.

Clown Box: Clown hair - Burnt Sienna "S" strokes. Ruffle/pom-pom/dots/moon - Cadmium Yellow Medium. Star - Prussian Blue + Titanium White.

Horse: Blanket/halter - thin Cadmium Red Medium. Eye/hooves - Ivory Black. Spots/stirrup - Titanium White + Ivory Black. Pull string - Titanium White + Burnt Umber with tiny Burnt Umber lines.

Ball: Sections - Cadmium Red, Terra Verte, Prussian Blue. Lines - Cadmium Yellow Medium.

Bunny: Eyes - Ivory Black. Ribbon - Flesh Tint + Cadmium Red Medium (3:1).

Doll: Scarf - Ivory Black - Titanium White + Ivory Black (3:1) highlights. Arms - Raw Umber shading. Skirt - Cadmium Red Medium shading. Apron - Dioxazine Purple shading - detail with Cadmium Yellow Medium and Titanium White.

Mouse: Ear/nose - Flesh Tint. Eye - Ivory Black.

# STEP 4

Letter the list with a fine point pen. Shade with Raw Umber.

Base Santa Claus and treats with a light coat of the following acrylic colors:

Hi-Lite Flesh: face
Neutral Grey: beard and cookie plate
Sable Brown: cookies
Violet Haze: hat fur, sleeves, coat edge
Tomato Red: hat, coat, pants, sock stripes
Deep Teal: mittens, sock stripes

# STEP 6

Add fine details with a liner. Thin the paint with odorless thinner as needed.

Face features: Eyelash line - Burnt Umber. Eye/nose - Flesh Tint + Burnt Sienna shading. Hat line - Burnt Sienna shading. Beard/mustache - Titanium White fine line highlights - Titanium White + Ivory Black darker shading.

Santa's treats: Milk - Titanium White + Ivory Black (3:1). Glass highlights/cookie plate trim - Titanium White. Cookies - Titanium White + a touch Burnt Umber highlights - Burnt Umber shading.

Fur: Titanium White + Dioxazine Purple + a touch Ivory Black tiny brush stroke textured shading - Titanium White highlights.

Socks: Terra Verte + Titanium White (3:1) fuzzy texture lines on green stripes.

# STEP 5

Shade and highlight Santa with the following alkyds, thinning the paint as needed:

Flesh Tint: Face/hat line/features - Flesh Tint + Titanium White (2:1). Hat line - deepen shading with Flesh Tint + Burnt Sienna (3:1).

Cadmium Red Medium: Suit/sock stripes - Cadmium Red Medium - shade with Cadmium Red Medium + Ivory Black (3:1) - highlight with Cadmium Red Medium + Cadmium Yellow Medium (2:1) + a touch Titanium White.

Terra Verte: Mittens/sock stripes - shade with Terra Verte + Ivory Black (3:1).

Titanium White: Glass - Titanium White. Beard/mustache lines and cookie plate - thin Titanium White + Ivory Black (3:1).

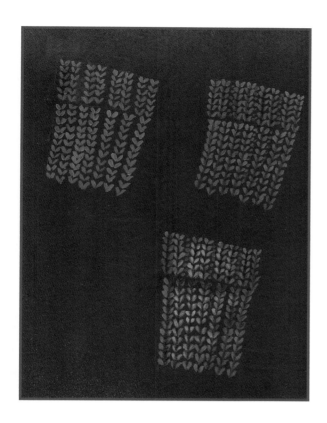

# STEP 7

Paint the knitted stocking background. Mix Terra Verte + Prussian Blue (3:1). Add Titanium White to the mix to make three separate values.

With a liner and the medium value color, make two strokes in a V shape. Create the knitted look with continuous vertical rows of strokes.

Use the dark value to make a thin line through the center of each V row. Use the light value to highlight some of the Vs. Let dry.

Shade the stocking with Ivory Black.

# FINISHING

Spray the finished ornament with varnish. Hang the chain and charms over the satin cording and wrap around the hanger loop

Glue Santa's list in place. Glue the elf on top and the chosen toys in place, using styrofoam to fill in the body of the stocking.

*And to all*
*a good night ...*

# Contact Information

LYNNE ANDREWS
ANDREWS181@COX.NET
WWW.LYNNEANDREWS.COM

HELAN BARRICK
BARRICKMDA@AOL.COM
WWW.HELANBARRICK.COM

TRUDY BEARD
TRUDY@TRUDYBEARDDESIGNS.COM
WWW.TRUDYBEARDDESIGNS.COM

MARGOT CLARK
MARGOT@MARGOTCLARK.COM
WWW.MARGOTCLARK.COM

DEBBIE COTTON
SIMPLYCOTTON@XPLORNET.COM
WWW.SIMPLY-COTTON.COM

HEIDI ENGLAND
HEIDI@HEIDIENGLAND.COM
WWW.HEIDIENGLAND.COM

CYNTHIA EREKSON
INFO@QUILTEDACORN.COM
WWW.QUILTEDACORN.COM

PEGGY HARRIS
PEGGY@PEGGYHARRIS.COM
WWW.PEGGYHARRIS.COM

KAREN HUBBARD
MAPAHUB@COMCAST.NET
WWW.HUBBARDSCUPBOARDPACKETS.COM

JO SONJA JANSEN
FOLKART@JOSONJA.COM
WWW.JOSONJA.NET

ANDY JONES
ANDYJONES@DECORATIVEARTSCOLLECTION.ORG
WWW.DECORATIVEARTSCOLLECTION.ORG

MARY JO LEISURE
MJL@MARYJOLEISURE.COM
WWW.MARYJOLEISURE.COM

ARLENE LINTON
LINTONAC@AOL.COM
WWW.RAINBOWSBEGINNING.COM

SHARON MCNAMARA-BLACK
SALES@SETTLERSCABIN.COM
WWW.SETTLERSCABIN.COM

DEB MALEWSKI
DEBMALEWSKI@SBCGLOBAL.NET
WWW.DEBMALEWSKI.COM

TONI MCGUIRE
TONIMC@APEX.NET

JO AVIS MOORE
JOAVISMOOREMDA@COX.NET

TINA SUE NORRIS
TINADESIGNS@COMPORIUM.NET
WWW.TINADESIGNS.COM

GOLDA RADER
RADERIZMS@HUGHES.NET
WWW.RADERIZMS.BLOGSPOT.COM

SHARA REINER
SHARA@ANGELTHYME.COM
WWW.ANGELTHYME.COM

PEGGY STOGDILL
PAINTING@PEGGYSTOGDILL.COM
WWW.PEGGYSTOGDILL.COM

MAXINE THOMAS
STIPPLER@AOL.COM
WWWW.COUNTRYPRIMATIVES.NET

ROSEMARY WEST
ROSEMARYWEST@SUDDENLINK.COM

SHIRLEY WILSON
WWW.LADYBUGART.COM

## Ornaments courtesy of

CABIN CRAFTERS (WOODEN ORNAM...)
PO BOX 270
NEVADA, IA 50201
PHONE: 800-669-3920
WWW.CABINCRAFTERS.COM

DELLA & COMPANY (TIN ORNAMENTS)
5208 LAKE CHARLES
WACO, TX 76710
PHONE: 254-772-6927
WWW.DELLAANDCOMPANY.COM

PORCELAIN TREASURES (PORCELAIN ORNAMENTS)
3446 MCCUTCHEON RD.
COLUMBUS, OH 43230
PHONE: 614-417-7407
PORCELAINLADY@WEBTV.NET

# THE DECORATIVE ARTS COLLECTION MUSEUM

The Decorative Arts Collection Museum has been forward thinking in its strategy from its inception in 1982.

With a two-pronged approach, a collection has been assembled that showcases both the historic roots and the contemporary direction of decorative painting.

The historic portion of the works has outstanding examples of early-American painted tin. Other fine pieces illustrate the variety of decorative painting: frakturs, theorems, stenciling, Chippendale painting, and pith paintings—to mention a few. The Collection also features a variety of folk art from around the globe, and contains a wide variety of mediums and an incredible diversity of surfaces.

Developing the historic portion of the Collection is an on-going process with a continuous search for additional fine examples of artwork to augment the current body of works.

The resurgence in decorative painting in the late 1940s and 1950s helped to form the foundation of the contemporary collection. The Museum is pleased to have pieces from some of the early painters who shared their knowledge and brought the art form to the masses. These artists developed new techniques and their own unique style of painting. Pioneering artists, such as Peter Hunt and Peter Ompir, inspired many people to take brush in hand and begin painting. In keeping with the our mission, one of the primary goals is the continuation of public education about decorative painting and the techniques used to create these masterworks.

The Decorative Arts Collection Museum is the premier repository of decorative painting. This heritage must be cared for and preserved. Your participation is vital to the success of our mission and we welcome your support and partnership in this worthwhile endeavor. This is the art form you love—that is important to you. Join us in making certain that future generations will also be able to see the treasures of our collection. Seriously consider becoming a Friend of the museum today—for today and for tomorrow.

DECORATIVE ARTS COLLECTION MUSEUM
404-627-3662
WWW.DECORATIVEARTSCOLLECTION.ORG

# Some Highlights from the Collection ...

# Order these fine publications from the Decorative Arts Collection Museum

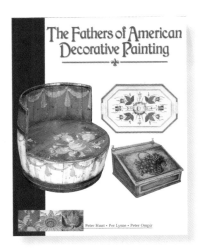

**FATHERS OF AMERICAN DECORATIVE PAINTING**
- 32 PAGES
- SOFT COVER
- BIOGRAPHIES OF PETER HUNT, PER LYSNE, AND PETER OMPIR AND PHOTOS OF THEIR WORK (NO INSTRUCTIONS, NO PATTERNS)
- $10.00 + S&H

Call or click to place your order for these fantastic books from the Decorative Arts Collection Museum.

Remember, every order helps to support the museum's mission of collection, preservation, and education.

The Decorative Arts Collection Museum
PO Box 18028
Atlanta, GA 30316
404-627-3662
www.decorativeartscollection.org

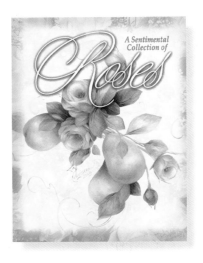

**A SENTIMENTAL COLLECTION OF ROSES**
- CD-ROM ONLY
- 24 ROSE LESSONS WITH PATTERNS
- PHOTOGRAPHS OF 88 ROSE PAINTINGS BY YOUR FAVORITE ARTISTS
- $24.95 + S&H

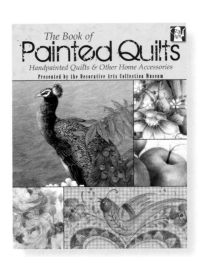

**THE BOOK OF PAINTED QUILTS**
- 166 PAGES
- HARDCOVER
- 14 QUILTS
- 14 COMPANION PROJECTS
- COMPLETE INSTRUCTIONS, PATTERNS, AND QUILTING DIAGRAMS
- $24.95 + S&H

**PAINTED TREASURES**
- 144 PAGES
- HARDCOVER WITH DUST JACKET
- 16 PROJECTS
- GALLERY OF IMAGES FROM THE MUSEUM'S COLLECTION OF ART WORK
- $29.95 + S&H

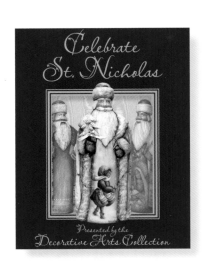

**CELEBRATE ST. NICHOLA**
- 144 PAGES
- HARDCOVER WITH DUST JACKET
- 24 PROJECTS
- 43 HANDPAINTED SANTA FIGURINES
- $34.95 + S&H